The Vercelli Book f. 133

METHUEN'S OLD ENGLISH LIBRARY

General Editors

A. H. Smith
F. Norman

★

CYNEWULF'S *ELENE*

Methuen's Old English Library

General Editors: A. H. Smith, Quain Professor of English, University College, London; and F. Norman, Professor of German, King's College, London

Poetry

THE DREAM OF THE ROOD
Edited by Bruce Dickins, Elrington and Bosworth Professor of Anglo-Saxon in the University of Cambridge; and Alan S. C. Ross, Professor of Linguistics in the University of Birmingham.

THE BATTLE OF MALDON
Edited by E. V. Gordon. With a Frontispiece and a map.

JUDITH
Edited by B. J. Timmer, Queen Mary College, London.

WALDERE
Edited by F. Norman.

DEOR
Edited by Kemp Malone, Professor of English,
Johns Hopkins University.

JULIANA
Edited by Rosemary Woolf, University of Hull.

Prose

THE PARKER CHRONICLE: 832–900
Edited by A. H. Smith.

ÆLFRIC'S COLLOQUY
Edited by G. N. Garmonsway, Reader in English,
King's College, London.

SERMO LUPI AD ANGLOS
Edited by Dorothy Whitelock,
Fellow of St. Hilda's College, Oxford.

Studies

EARLY MIDDLE ENGLISH LITERATURE
By R. M. Wilson, Professor of English Language,
University of Sheffield.

MIDDLE ENGLISH LITERATURE
By George Kane, Professor of English, Royal Holloway College,
London.

THE LOST LITERATURE OF MEDIEVAL ENGLAND
By R. M. Wilson, Professor of English Language,
University of Sheffield.

AN OLD ENGLISH GRAMMAR
By Randolph Quirk, Reader in English, University of Durham;
and C. L. Wrenn, Rawlinson and Bosworth Professor of Anglo-Saxon
in the University of Oxford.

CYNEWULF'S
ELENE

EDITED BY

P. O. E. GRADON,
PH.D., M.A.

Fellow of St Hugh's College, Oxford

METHUEN & CO LTD
36 ESSEX STREET · STRAND · LONDON WC2

First published 1958

107640

Catalogue No. 7725/U

© *1958 Notes and Introduction P. O. E. Gradon*

Printed in Great Britain
by Butler & Tanner Ltd, Frome and London

PREFACE

THE aim of this edition has been to sift the mass of criticism, emendation and speculation which has grown up round the text. In order to bring the work into conformity with the requirements of the series in which it is published it has been necessary in view of the length of the text to reduce the apparatus to a minimum; but it is hoped that the bibliography will afford sufficient guidance to the considerable literature on the text.

The editor has pleasure in acknowledging the help received from the Bodleian Library and the Cambridge University Library; to whose courtesy she is indebted for photostats of Marsh 13 and MS Mm. 6. 4 respectively. She also wishes to thank the Prefect of the Vatican Library for providing photostats of Vatican MS Graec. 2048 and the Librarian of the St Gall Stiftsbibliothek for photostats of St Gall MS 225. To the authorities of the British Museum she owes thanks for their invariable courtesy and in particular to Dr Cyril Moss of the department of Oriental Printed Books and Manuscripts for his very generous help in checking the collation of the Syriac versions of the *Inventio Crucis* from the originals.

The editor's thanks are also due to Canonîco Marinone, Archivist of the Eusebian Archives at Vercelli, for enabling her to collate the manuscript, to the Worshipful Masters of the Bench for permission to consult Maier's transcript and the correspondence of Charles Purton Cooper in the Library at Lincoln's Inn, and to the Deputy Keeper of the Records for permission to consult the records of the issue of the Appendices of Cooper's Report on Rymer's *Foedera*. The research in which the book originated was aided by a grant from the Central Research Fund of the University of London, which enabled her to visit Vercelli to see the manuscript.

Dr Kenneth Brooks and Mr Neil Ker have contributed materially to the work; the former by the loan of his manuscript edition of *Andreas* and by many helpful suggestions; the latter by drawing the editor's attention to the presence at

Lincoln's Inn of Maier's transcript. Unfortunately Mr Ker's *Catalogue of MSS containing Anglo-Saxon,* to which the editor is also indebted, came to hand too late to be included in the bibliography. The set of Ἐκκλησιαζτικὴ Ἀλήθεια used in the discussion of the source she owes to the kindness of Canon J. A. Douglas to whom it belongs. Finally the editor wishes to thank Professor C. L. Wrenn for the interest sustained since the work's inception in 1944.

OXFORD
1956

CONTENTS

ABBREVIATIONS

AEW	F. Holthausen, *Altenglisches Etymologisches Wörterbuch*
AfdA	*Anzeiger für deutsches Alterthum*
Anglia Beibl . . .	*Anglia Beiblatt*
Archiv	(*Herrigs*) *Archiv für das Studium der neueren Sprachen u. Literaturen*
BB	*Bonner Beiträge zur Anglistik*
BT, BTS	J. Bosworth and T. N. Toller, *An Anglo-Saxon Dictionary* and Supplement
Bülbring	K. D. Bülbring, *Altenglisches Elementarbuch*
BZ	*Byzantinische Zeitschrift*
EETS	Early English Text Society
EPNS	Publications of the English Place Name Society
ESt	*Englische Studien*
Gött. gel. Anz. . .	*Göttingische gelehrte Anzeigen*
Grein-Köhler . . .	C. W. M. Grein, *Sprachschatz der ags. Dichter* revised G. Köhler
HBS	Henry Bradshaw Society
JEGPh	*Journal of English and Germanic Philology*
JJJ	E. A. Kock, *Jubilee Jaunts and Jottings*, Lunds Universitets Aarskrift, N.F. Pt. i, Vol. xiv (2)
Lindisf.	Lindisfarne Gospels
MGH	*Monumenta Germaniae Historica*, ed. G. Pertz
MLA	Publications of the Modern Language Association of America
MLN	*Modern Language Notes*
MLR	*Modern Language Review*
MPh	*Modern Philology*
NED	*New English Dictionary*
PBB	*Beiträge zur Geschichte der deutschen Sprache un· Literatur*, ed. H. Paul and W. Braune
PL	*Patrologiae cursus completus;* series latina, ed. J. P. Migne

R¹	*Rushworth Gospels*, Matthew, Mark 1–2, 15; John 18, 1–3
R²	ib. Mark and John except as above, Luke
RES	*Review of English Studies*
Ritual	Durham Ritual
RS	Rolls Series
Sievers-Brunner . .	E. Sievers, *Angelsächsische Grammatik*, revised K. Brunner
VPs	*Vespasian Psalter*
Wright-Wülcker . .	*Anglo-Saxon and English Vocabularies*, revised R. P. Wülcker
ZfdA	*Zeitschrift für deutsches Alterthum*
ZfdPh	*Zeitschrift für deutsche Philologie*

INTRODUCTION

I. HISTORY AND DESCRIPTION OF THE TEXT

THE manuscript of *Elene*, the Vercelli Book, is now No. CXVII in the Eusebian Archives at Vercelli in northern Italy.[1] The manuscript consists of 136 leaves of thin parchment each of which has from 23 to 33 lines of writing. The last folio has been left blank while others, in each case the concluding folio of an item, are only partly filled. Each leaf is about 20 by 31 centimetres in size. Ruled lines and margins appear on both recto and verso folios. *Elene* follows Homily xxii and extends from f. 121 to f. 133^b. *Elene* and the following homily on St Guthlac together form the eighteenth and nineteenth gatherings of the manuscript, the eighteenth gathering extending from f. 121 to f. 128 and the nineteenth from f. 129 to f. 135. The last leaf has been attached to the back of gathering XIX. These gatherings have been marked and numbered, probably in a later hand, by placing at the head of the first page of each a roman numeral, and at the foot of the last page of each one of the letters of the alphabet from A to T. Damage to the manuscript seems to have obliterated the letter T at the end of gathering XIX, but the letter S is visible on f. 128^b and the numerals xviii and xix on ff. 121, 129.

There are numerous tears and holes. Small holes appear in the text of *Elene* on f. 131^b above *hrusan* 1091; on f. 131 above the *s* of *piðsóc* 1039 and in many other instances. These sometimes damage a letter in the text although in no case do they affect legibility. Such holes appear on f. 122 in the *e* of *róde* 103; on 124^b in the first *ȝ* of *ȝinȝne* 353; on f. 127^b in the *e* of *piðsǽcest* 663 and so on. But the reagent, used with such disastrous results in some parts of the manuscript, has not affected the text of *Elene*.[2] The large oval stain after *fór* on

---

[1] For accounts of the manuscript see p. 76.

[2] Cp f. 54^a. Examination of the manuscript shows that the stain which appears to cover part of *Fates* 96–122 has destroyed the writing. Only the writing on the other side can now be seen. The letters *Pa?*, read by Maier in line 100, appear to be the *ær* of *mæran* on the other side.

f. 121 just covers, but does not obscure, the final stroke of the *r*. But many pages show discoloration and smudging. Folio 125, in particular, is stained and blotted although the text is legible. The parchment on f. 125ᵇ is badly discoloured. The numerous tears and holes in the margins, many of them repaired by the Vatican in 1913, do not affect the text's legibility.

The handwriting is a tenth-century Anglo-Irish hand from the south of England. Keller supposed the manuscript to have been written between 960 and 980. Förster, on the other hand, thinks it impossible to date so precisely, since the character of handwriting depends partly on the scribe's age and the conventions of his scriptorium. In the Vercelli Book, the comparative accuracy and regularity of the script suggest an experienced scribe and Förster, therefore, dates rather less precisely than Keller in the second half of the tenth century.[1] As evidence of a date at the beginning of this period he notes that Latin words are written in insular script and not, as became usual towards the end of the tenth century, in Frankish cursive. There are no grounds for assuming that the manuscript is in more than one hand although the writing becomes noticeably smaller on f. 131ᵇ after *ȝodȝimmas*.[2]

The manuscript is plain in appearance although ornamental capitals introduce homilies xix and xxi and line 1478 of *Andreas*. These have been shown by Wormald to derive from types found in MS Junius 27.[3] On ff. 47ᵇ and 51 the roundels of the capitals are filled or partly filled with a scallop pattern thought by Förster to be reminiscent of Irish work. One or more plain capitals introduce each homily and each lection of the poems. Only in *Elene* are the lections numbered. The cover, which dates from the nineteenth century, is of tooled leather and has on the spine in black letters: *Homiliarum Liber ignoti idiomatis* | 41 | Secolo x | cxvii.

---

[1] See Keller, *Palaestra* xliii. 33, 39–40; Förster, *Codice Vercellese* 11–14.

[2] Cp Wülcker, *Codex Vercellensis* vii; Napier, ZfdA xxxiii. 67. Later additions are noted in the textual variants. For marginal additions see Krapp, *Vercelli Book* xv–xvi; Sisam, *Studies in the History of Old English Literature* 109–18.

[3] *Archaeologia* xci. 120, 134.

History of the Text

The origin of the Vercelli Book is unknown. The language of the codex contributes little to a solution of the problem, since few features are common to the whole.[1] The spelling *-et* for *-eþ* in verbal forms is Anglian and Kentish, but its occurrence is sporadic.[2] Forms such as *ʒionlic, camwerod, camrædenne, ʒeonsiðe* (MS. ʒeon, on siðe), *lansceare, ʒirsandæʒ* may be Kentish since comparable forms occur, for instance, in the Kentish gloss in Vespasian D vi, the Canterbury Psalter and Textus Roffensis. But comparable forms occur in late West Saxon texts also.[3] The most common features of the manuscript spelling are the diphthong *io* and the doubling and shortening of consonants. The latter is late Old English, the former Kentish or early West Saxon, but such spellings are more frequent in the homilies than in the poems. They could be due to the use of a Kentish or West Saxon homiliary for part of the collection. But in view of the sprinkling of probably Kentish forms they may rather represent the lapses of a Kentishman writing the West Saxon *koine*.[4] Briefly, the language of the manuscript is at best an equivocal witness. More suggestive are the parallels between the Vercelli Book and the Exeter Book, which in view of its resemblance to MS Lambeth 149, is held to be of western provenance.[5] But the significance of these parallels is also

---

[1] Förster believed that the language indicated a connection with St Mary's, Worcester, and he refers to striking similarities between the language of the Vercelli Book and Wulfgeat's manuscripts of Wulfstan's homilies. But the dialect blend noted by Dunkhase can be otherwise explained.

[2] See f. 62 4; f. 110 20; *Soul and Body* 105, 132. Cp Sievers-Brunner § 357 n3. But cp Schlemilch, *Sprachdenkmäler der Übergangszeit* 56–7.

[3] f. 62 20, f. 83ᵇ 14; f. 112ᵇ 12; *Andreas*, 4, 501; f. 73ᵇ 17. Brotanek, Anglia Beibl xxvi. 235. Cp Luick § 677.

[4] Cp Sisam, *Studies* 153. The unrounding of *y* (which is primarily although not quite exclusively Kentish) occurs in *wyrðmendo* f. 89ᵇ 24; *wyrðment* f. 116 30–1; *ʒefellan* f. 16 15; *ʒeðeldelice* f. 5ᵇ 17; *ʒerene* f. 88 20; cp *acynned = acenned* f. 86ᵇ 13. Possibly Kentish is the peculiar spelling *dieorwyrðum* f. 70 6 but most probably it represents an attempted correction of *io* to *eo*.

[5] A miscellany somewhat parallel in content to the Exeter Book is mentioned in a medieval catalogue from Glastonbury: *Vita Sancti*

3

ambiguous. Thus both have the *Soul and Body* poem, but the appearance of *Azarias* in both the Exeter Book and the Cædmon Manuscript warns against the easy assumption that similarity of content proves identity of origin; both manuscripts have signed poems of Cynewulf; but a common place of origin for the two manuscripts presupposes a shared manuscript or manuscripts of Cynewulf's poetry. The choice of two Cynewulfian poems apiece for each codex might then be thought strangely arbitrary. There are the curious parallels between Vercelli homily x and *The Wanderer* but these may be due to the use of a common source. Both the Vercelli Book and the Exeter Book have lives of St Guthlac, but the cult of the saint had probably spread beyond Mercia by the tenth century. This is implied by the varied provenance of the manuscripts of Felix of Crowland's Life (notably C.C.C.C. 389, a Canterbury book); by the frequent appearance of his festival in ecclesiastical calendars [1] of varied provenance; by the existence of a proper mass for the saint in the Missal of Robert of Jumièges, thought by the Henry Bradshaw Society editor to be a Winchester book but possibly South-Western in origin.[2] His cult may have spread from a western centre such as Glastonbury, Worcester or Hereford [3] and was perhaps partly due to an association between the austerity of the eremitical life and the new monasticism.[4]

Gutlaci et liber Pronosticorum & de animabus defunctorum & de ultima resurrexione et aenigmata multorum (John of Glastonbury's Chronicle, ed. Hearne 436).

[1] See Wormald, *English Calendars before 1100* (HBS lxxii) esp. nos. 3, 5–7, 10–14, 16, 17. These entries, although no doubt in part martyrological only, contrast strongly with the very limited incidence of, for example, St Pega, who amongst the calendars cited, appears only in Douce 296 and Lambeth 873 probably both Crowland books (cp N. R. Ker, *Medieval Libraries of Great Britain*). She appears in the probably Mercian Martyrology. (Cp Felix' *Life of Guthlac* ed. Colgrave (9–10) which was not available before this book went to press.)

[2] Ed. Wilson (HBS xi). Cp Sisam, *Studies* 9. A proper mass for the saint appears also in Vitellius A xviii (Warren, Leofric Missal 303–4).

[3] Offices for the saint appear in the 13 c. Hereford Breviary (HBS xl) and fragments in C.C.C.C. 198, a Worcester book (cp N. R. Ker, *op. cit.*).   [4] Cp Bishop, *The Bosworth Psalter* 23.

There seems therefore no cogent reason for associating the Vercelli Book with the west. The Glastonbury Calendar indeed which seems to have been the basis of both the calendar in the Leofric Missal and the calendar in the Bosworth Psalter,[1] a Canterbury book, may well serve to remind us that ecclesiastical as well as linguistic affinities are significant for manuscript origins. Perhaps further research on the origin of the Vercelli Book might usefully start from the hypothesis that it is a Winchester or Canterbury book (perhaps with Glastonbury antecedents) rather than a Worcester one as Förster thought.[2]

The Vercelli Codex may have been given its present form by the scribe. The collection does not follow the church calendar but is a series of penitential homilies covering mainly the traditional themes of meditation: *Mors tua, mors domini, nota culpe, gaudia celi*. That the collection is composite may be suggested by the appearance of the numbers ii, iii, iiii, v, vi preceding homilies VII–XI. Had this numbering represented merely the numbering of the homilies in relation to the Fates of the Apostles we might have expected the number i before homily VI which immediately follows the Fates of the Apostles.[3] Instead the number xvi heads this homily representing possibly an old quire signature. The apparent lack of a number i in that case is, perhaps, due to its having appeared at the end of the concluding item of quire xv of the exemplar.[4]

[1] See Bishop, *The Bosworth Psalter.*

[2] It is interesting to notice that the sign $x\eth$ which appears in the Vercelli Book is common in Canterbury manuscripts. Cp Sisam, *Studies* 109–10. The resemblance between the capital on f. 49 of the Vercelli Book and the capitals in the Junius Manuscript is also suggestive but Wormald has pointed out that this style is 'part of the common vocabulary of English illuminators of that time', *Archaeologia* xci. 119.

[3] But it is perhaps to be seen at the bottom of f. 54[b]. Cp Ker, *Catalogue of MSS*, p. 461.

[4] Another possible indication of mechanical copying appears on f. 109[b] where the scribe has left a blank for a capital which has in fact been supplied. The use of superscriptions and capitalization at the beginning of the items is haphazard by comparison with such a manuscript as, for example, Bodley 340/342 and may perhaps represent different scribal traditions, thus indicating the different components of the manuscript. For linguistic evidence see Peterson, *Studies in Philology* l. 559–65.

The collection cannot have been completed much before the middle of the ninth century since the eleventh homily refers to the Danish invasions. The use of apocryphal material in the fifteenth and twenty-second homilies suggests a tenth-century date, for the Blickling Homilies, the Homilies attributed to Wulfstan, and Ælfric's preface to the Catholic Homilies all witness an interest in apocryphal literature after about 900. Förster, moreover, calls attention to references to the end of the world in homilies xi and xv. Some of the prose material in the codex may, thus, date from the ninth or tenth century, but more probably from the tenth, while the whole codex may represent either the autograph of the collector or an apograph.

How the manuscript came to Vercelli is not known. Dr Sisam, however, has shown that the fragment of a psalm with neums on f. 24[b] suggests that the manuscript was at Vercelli already in the eleventh century although it was still in England when a hand later than the scribe's wrote *writ thus* on f. 63b, *sclean* on f. 99 and scribbles on the last folio.[1] It is thus possible to discount both the view of Neigebaur that the manuscript was taken to Vercelli at the time of the Renaissance and the Cardinal Guala theory first put forward in 1844. Whether Vercelli in fact possessed a hostel for English pilgrims as Wülcker thought or whether the manuscript was taken to Vercelli by Bishop Ulf of Dorchester may be doubted but since Vercelli was on the main pilgrim route to Rome the possibilities are evidently numerous.

The first certain reference to the codex is in a letter written in 1748 from the bibliophile, Giuseppe Bianchini of Verona, to Cardinal Vittorio delle Lancie. In this letter he not only describes the manuscript but transcribes a passage, which, for all its errors, is clearly taken from ff. 85[b]–86 of the Vercelli Book.[2] Bianchini's discovery, however, attracted little attention and

---

[1] Sisam, *Studies* 109–18.

[2] See G. de-Gregory, *Istoria della Vercellese Letteratura ed Arti* iv. 554–60. Förster also draws attention to the entry *Liber Gothicus sive Longobardus* in an inventory of 1602. This book, although numbered XC, may have been the Vercelli Book.

the manuscript became widely known only after its rediscovery in the early nineteenth century.

In the years 1821–3, the jurist Friedrich Blume made a tour of Italian libraries to collect material for his study of roman law. Between October 27 and November 19 of 1822 he examined the chapter library at Vercelli where, among other manuscripts, he inspected the Vercelli Book, which he says contains 'Legenden oder Homilien in "angelsäxischer Sprache" '.[1] The news of the discovery soon spread in England and Germany. Blume spoke of it to the German antiquary Lappenberg who, on September 18 1832, wrote to Charles Purton Cooper telling him of Blume's discovery and referring him to a forthcoming description of it in the *Rheinisches Museum* by Jacob Grimm.[2] Negotiations followed with a view to borrowing the manuscript or making a copy [3] and Cooper having obtained a specimen of the homilies, sent it to Thorpe who confirmed that the language was 'saxon'.[4] The problem of seeing the manuscript had been solved meantime. The German antiquary, Warnkönig, having seen the account in the *Rheinisches Museum*,[5] writes to Cooper suggesting that a transcription should be made by Mone of Karlsruhe [6] and, upon his refusing, by Maier.[7] Maier left for Vercelli on October 15 1833 and appears to have completed his task in the spring of the following year.[8] The work was sent to Cooper, who was planning to print some of the manuscript as an appendix to the Report on Rhymer's *Foedera* with which he was concerned as secretary of the Record Commission. At Thorpe's suggestion he decided to print all the verse [9] and Thorpe was asked to undertake the edition. The work seems to have been well advanced

---

[1] *Iter Italicum* i. 87, 99.

[2] Correspondence of Charles Purton Cooper iii. 104. The correspondence is now in the Library at Lincoln's Inn. [3] *ib.* iv. 117, 126–9.

[4] *ib.* iv. 238, 273. Cooper seems to have sent specimens to Kemble also. See Correspondence v.248.

[5] *Rheinisches Museum für Jurisprudenz* iv. 233.

[6] Correspondence iv. 290. [7] *ib.* iv. 298.

[8] *ib.* v. 322, 323. The transcript is now in the Library of Lincoln's Inn. Cp Ker, *Medium Aevum* xix. 17–25.

[9] *ib.* v. 463.

by 1835 [1] but the edition never appeared, for the Record Commission expired in 1837 and its report was not made. The appendices were stored and issued between July 8 1869 and October 10 1917 by the Record Office, which ordered that copies should be distributed in such a manner 'as may render them most useful for literary and historical purposes'.[2] A few copies, however, may have been distributed before 1869 and this is of interest for the history of the text, since Thorpe's work formed the basis of the early editions. Förster points out that Lappenberg seems to have received a copy, which he lent to Grimm who states in his preface that he made it the basis of his edition of *Andreas und Elene*, published in 1840.[3] Förster suggests that Lappenberg may have owed this copy to Thorpe, who was preparing a translation of Lappenberg's *Geschichte von England*. Grimm's edition was thus based on Thorpe's edition of Maier's transcript. Kemble's edition of 1843 seems to have been based partly on Grimm.[4] The first complete edition of all the verse in the codex was due to Grein but he, too, based his text on Thorpe, that is to say, on Maier's transcript.[5] Zupitza's

[1] Correspondence vi. 392.

[2] A list of recipients and details of distribution can be found in the *Printed Records Publications* of the Public Record Office i. 82; ii. 157, 158, 399.

[3] I have been unable to find any record of an issue of appendices A, B and C in one volume before 1869 although a copy of appendix B, which contains the text of *Elene*, was sent to Thorpe on November 23 1853. That Thorpe was accessible before that date is suggested by Grimm (*Andreas und Elene* p. iv) and by Kemble (*Poetry of the Codex Vercellensis* I v.). It may be suggested also by the existence at Lincoln's Inn of a second transcript signed *M.A.T. scripsit Ealing prope Londinium* 1835. The address and the initials suggest that it was made by one of Thorpe's family. Except for the runic passage from *Fates of the Apostles*, it contains the prose only and refers the reader to appendices B and D of Cooper's Report for the verse.

[4] See *Poetry of the Codex Vercellensis* I vi–vii.

[5] See Grein, *Bibliothek der ags. Poesie* i. 364. The inaccessibility of the manuscript vitiated some of the early discussion of the text, especially the cruces in line 580 where Thorpe, Grimm, Kemble and Grein read *awundrad* for MS *apundrad* and 1028 where they read *æðelu anbroce* for MS *æðelu anbręce*. Maier has the correct reading in 1028 and apparently *ápundrað* in 580 although the letters þ and p are difficult to distinguish in the transcript.

edition of 1877 was the first text of *Elene* to be based on a fresh inspection of the manuscript, its basis being a collation made by Professor P. Knöll of Vienna. All the poetry was collated by Wülcker for his revision of Grein. Other editors have used the collations of Napier or the facsimiles of Wülcker and Förster.

2. LANGUAGE OF THE TEXT

A linguistic analysis of the text of *Elene* suggests the following conclusions :

A. Certain features in the text are late West Saxon and are, therefore, scribal, since other evidence precludes so late a date. The most important of these forms are:

1. late WS smoothing appears in *ȝeseh* 841; *apehte* 304; *bepehte* 1298. These forms could, also, be Kentish or West Mercian, both dialects showing sporadic examples [1] (Bülbring § 313).

2. late palatal influence appears in *folcscere* 402; *ȝere* 859. Such forms are common in late WS (Bülbring § 314).

3. *frumpa* in 345 shows late *u* for *y*.

4. confusion of *u* and *eo* in *piðpeorpon* 294 (Luick § 286).

5. *e* in *hæftnede* 297; *preanedum* 883; *perodleste* 63 etc may be due to a non-WS mutation of *ea* or to late WS shift of stress in diphthongs (Luick §§ 265, 266). Possibly due to the latter is *prohtherd* 494.[2] Cp *Andreas* 1133, 1213, 671.

6. *morðorslehtes* in 650 and forms such as *perȝðu* 211; *ermðum* 767; *herpdon* 387 etc may, also, show non-WS mutations but Ælfric's works show comparable forms [3] (Bülbring § 179 n.i).

7. *lixtan* 23 etc has *i* for earlier *ie*.

8. late WS labialization and delabialization are common throughout the poem.

9. *-an* for *-on* in *samnodan* 19; *lixtan* 23 etc.

10. *pane* for *pone* in 294.

---

[1] Cp *siȝe becna* with the *a* above the line in 974.
[2] Cp Schlemilch, *op. cit.* 24–6.
[3] Cp. Cosijn, *Altwestsächsische Gramm.* i § 14.

11. *-an/ -on* for *-en* in *ʒecyðan* 409; *piston?* 459 etc. But these may be dialectal forms.[1]

12. *-ade* for *-ode* in *locade* 87 etc. These are characteristically Anglian but occur also in late WS.

13. *-o* for *-u* in *snyttro* 154; *brimo* 971 etc.

14. irregular lack of syncope in *pereʒan* 357; *modcpaniʒe* 377 etc.

15. simplification of double consonants in *hetend(um)* 18, 119;[2] *niða* 503 etc; and lengthening of consonants in *fricʒʒan* 157; *bissceophad* 1211 etc (Luick §§ 667 ff).[3]

16. loss of final guttural in *pliti* 89. Such forms are common in Kentish glosses but occur in late WS also; cp the back spelling *reonian* for *reoniʒan* in 833.

17. loss of initial *ʒ* in *eorne* 322; *eáre* 399. This is characteristic of late southern texts (Sievers-Brunner § 212 n.2).

18. *þan næʒlan* for *þam næʒlum* in 1127.

19. *feale* for *feala* in 636?

20. *snyttro* is invariable in the singular.

B. The text shows some features common in early (Alfredian) WS. The most important of these are:

1. *meaht* 511; *meahton* 166 etc. These are either early WS or Kentish.

2. The diphthong *ie* in *dierne* 1080; and in *ʒeieped* 102; *hiehða* 1086.

3. the spelling *ie* for *i* in *hiere* 222; *biesʒum(?)* 1244.[4] This spelling is characteristic of the Hatton MS of the *Pastoral Care*.

4. the form *deoʒol* in 1092 has been regarded as Mercian but

---

[1] See Sievers-Brunner § 365 & n.2.

[2] This form, however, may be due to the influence of the related forms *hatian, hete, hetol.* Cp Beo. 1828; *Orosius* ed. Sweet (EETS 79) 264.

[3] Cp Dunkhase, *Die Sprache der Wulfstan'schen Homilien* 68–9.

[4] The *i* in this word has been added above and slightly to the left of the *e*. Most editors, therefore, regard it as a correction not an addition and read *bisʒum.* But additions without a tag appear in 954 and 731 where the *l* of *halfa* and the *o* of *siʒora* have been added above the line in the same way. No deletion point is visible under the *e* but the traditional reading may, perhaps, be justified by reference to *Andreas* 1286 where the reading *pelle* is corrected by writing an *i* over the *e* without a deletion point.

similar forms without the characteristic WS diphthong occur also in the Hatton MS of the *Pastoral Care*.

5. *dyrndun* in 626 may be an early form.

6. the spelling *sð* for *st* occurs in *oferspiðesð* 93; *ʒetæhtesð* 1074; *ricesða* 1234. This spelling is characteristic of the Hatton MS of the *Pastoral Care*. Since this manuscript was commissioned by King Alfred for Worcester, it was presumably written in a West Saxon scriptorium in his reign. Moreover, the spelling occurs in at least one other manuscript which can be shown to be descended from an Alfredian original; namely, the Cotton manuscript of Gregory's Dialogues, which seems to have derived from a copy made for Bishop Wulfsige of Sherbourne.[1] It is, therefore, possible that the sporadic appearance of this spelling betrays an early West Saxon transcript.[2] But since there are no other instances of this spelling in the Vercelli Book, the forms in *Elene* are more probably due to a previous transcript of the poem than of the whole codex which, in any case, probably did not take shape until the tenth century.

7. *byrð* 1195. Syncopated verbal forms may have become generalized in the late ninth century in the Winchester area (cp Sisam, *Studies* 125).

C. Dialectal forms common to the whole codex are probably to be regarded as scribal. These are forms showing *a* before *l* + cons. and the spelling *io*. Other dialect forms are probably poetic and, therefore, give no indication of the provenance of the poem. These are:

1. forms with back mutation of *æ* such as *beaduróf* 152; *heaðofremmende* 130; *eatol* 901 etc.

2. forms with back mutation of *e* before a dental such as *meotod* 366 etc.

---

[1] Sisam, MLR xviii. 254–6. For the forms see *Prologus* 13, 15, 18, 19.

[2] It is, perhaps, worth noting that several manuscripts showing this spelling are associated with the south-west; for example, Exeter Book (*Juliana* 53); MS C.C.C.C. 41, a manuscript once at Exeter (*Sol. & Sat.* 22, 36, 18); Corpus MS of West Saxon Gospels from Bath (Matt. xi, 7; xxiv, 39; xxv, 44). For forms in Canterbury Psalter and Rule of St Benet cp Wildhagen, *Stud. z. engl. Phil.* xiii 208, 159–72; Hermanns, *Interlinearversion der Benediktinerregel* 100. Cp Sol. Sat. ed. Menner 16–17.

3. forms with *e* for WS *ǽ¹* such as *ʒeseʒe* 75; *neʒan* 287 etc.

4. reduplicating preterites as *heht* 42 etc; *leort* 1104.

D. Less common dialect forms, which may, in some cases, indicate the provenance of the poem, are:

1. irregular mutation in *præcmæcʒʒas* 387; *sæcʒ* ? 1256. Such mutations are frequent in Rushworth and Lindisf but not unknown in WS.

2. *stærcedfyrhðe* in 38 is probably Anglian.[1]

3. *ælfylce* in 36 may be Anglian but the prefix *-æl* occurs, also, in Hatton MS of the *Pastoral Care*.

4. *elda* 476; *heaðopelma* 579; *cearpelmum* 1257 represent forms occurring in Kentish, Saxon patois and sporadically in VPs.

5. second fronting appears in *hrefn* 110; *heremeðle* 550 etc. These are characteristically Kentish or West Mercian but occur sporadically in other dialects.

6. Anglian smoothing in *æht* 473.

7. (*feðe*)*ʒestas* 844 may be Anglian or Kentish.

8. (*puldor*)*ʒeofa* in 681 could be non-WS or Saxon patois.

9. *seolf* in 708 for late WS *sylf*.

10. *eorre* in 401 is Mercian and Saxon patois.

11. (*stan*)*ʒreopum* in 823 lacks the analogical restoration of *i* which is usual in WS.

12. *onsion* in 349 could be Northumbrian or Kentish but unmutated forms of this kind occur in Alfredian manuscripts.

13. Kentish or West Mercian fronting of *ǽ²* may occur in *elðes* ? 1294 and *stenan* ? 151.

14. Mercian confusion of *ð* and *d* in *ʒuðpearð* 14; *ʒehdum* 531; *elðes* ? 1294.

15. *ʒrinʒ* 115; *ʒrunʒon* 126; *æcleape* 321; *æclæca* 901 show confusion of *c* and *ʒ* which occurs occasionally in R¹ but, also, in WS.[2]

16. *ástah* 188; *dreah* 1260 have final unvoicing which is common in R¹ but also in later WS; cp *þurg* 289; 789.

---

[1] *æ* from mutation of *a* by retraction before *r* occurs in Northumbrian and in the Mercian Life of St Chad.

[2] Cp Campbell, *Battle of Brunanburh* 98, for the view that *crinʒan* and *ʒrinʒan* are from different roots.

17. West Mercian metathesis of *ðl* to *ld* in *spald* 300.[1]

18. nom. and acc. of personal pronoun appears in the plural as *heo* 116; 254; 382; *hio* 166, 324 etc; *he* 59, 68, 496.[2]

19. *hafu* in 807 and *pendo* ? 348.

20. *snyrȝan* for *snyrian* in 244.

21. *mid* with acc. in 275, 736, 997.

A linguistic analysis thus suggests that many features are late WS.[3] These presumably belong to the final stage of the history of the text, its incorporation in the collection represented by the Vercelli Book. Secondly, the poem shows some early features, some of them characteristic of the Hatton MS of the *Pastoral Care*, and the poem may at some time have existed in an early West Saxon form.[4] Finally, the balance of the occasional forms suggests a Mercian original. Of these the most significant is *spald*, the primacy of which is suggested by the metre, but the syntax and accidence of the poem would, also, support such a view.

The assumption that Cynewulf was a Mercian is confirmed by the metrical evidence. Most significant is the evidence of the leonine rhymes in the epilogue to which Sievers first drew attention.[5] These fall into three groups. Firstly, the rhymes *onwreah : fah* must be read as *onwrah : fah*. The form *onwrah* is more common in Anglian than in WS. Secondly, the forms *amæt : beȝeat* must be read as *amæt : beȝæt* or *amet : beȝet* if they are to rhyme.[6] The former would be non-WS; the latter would represent a second fronting dialect. Thirdly, the false rhymes *riht : ȝepeaht* and *miht : peaht* must be read as *ræht : ȝepæht* and *mæht : pæht* or *reht : ȝepeht* and *meht : peht*. The rhymes *mæht : pæht* would show Anglian smoothing of *ea*; the *e* readings smoothing of *ea* to *e*. The latter is common in late WS but such an origin is impossible here. The only alternative is Mercian. The smoothing of *ea* to *e* occurs in VPs in such forms

---

[1] *seld* occurs in VPs and the Life of St Chad. Cp EPNS xxvi map 8.

[2] Cp Sievers-Brunner § 334 n.2.

[3] These late forms often vitiate the metre; e.g. *elþeodiȝe* 57, 82; *stiðhidiȝe* 121; *bepundene* 733; *hetend(um)* 18, 119; *niða* 465, 503; *eare* 399; *eorne* 322.

[4] Cp Sisam, *Studies* 12.

[5] PBB ix. 235 n.i.　　　　[6] But see note to line 1247.

as *ʒepeht, bepehton, ʒepehte* and in R[1] in *ʒepehtunʒe*.[1] These rhymes, therefore, show only that the poet was Anglian.[2] The rhyme *ræht : ʒepæht*, on the other hand, could be only Northumbrian. Li. shows forms such as *cnæht*, but in other dialects the smoothing of *eo* is *e* and would give the form *reht*. If, therefore, it can be shown that the poet's dialect was not Northumbrian, the reading *reht* is necessary and the first rhyme is *reht : ʒepeht*. This would make probable a second rhyme *meht : peht* although *mæht : pæht*[3] would be possible. But the forms (*ʒe*)*peht* and *meht* are most probably West Mercian. The decision thus seems to lie between West Mercian and Northumbrian. That Northumbrian is, if not impossible, exceedingly improbable is suggested by the runic signature.

Sievers first noted that the poet's signature, fossilized in the acrostic, must represent the form which the poet was accustomed to use.[4] The variant *Cynwulf*, which occurs in *Crist* and the *Fates*, is current throughout the period, but the form *Cynewulf* must belong to a period during or after the transition of medial *i* to *e*. Since, moreover, the linguistic and metrical evidence suggests a Mercian or Northumbrian original, the evidence must be sought in dateable texts from these areas. The only available Northumbrian text, the *Liber Vitae* of the mid-ninth century, shows, in its many examples of the name, no form with medial *e*. It seems, therefore, that the evidence should be sought in Mercian texts. Dr Sisam has pointed out that the so-called Northumbrian genealogy, which Sievers used as evidence of *e* forms in Northumbrian, is, in fact, Mercian and witnesses the existence of *i/e* forms from the central midlands about the year 812.[5] The evidence of charters, upon which Sievers largely depended, is unreliable, since they are often preserved in later copies and their attribution may be untrust-

---

[1] But Lindisf and Ritual sometimes confuse *æ* and *e* and the smoothing of *ea* to *e* occurs sporadically in Kentish glosses.

[2] This conclusion is supported by the presumable rhymes *mæhte : cræfte* or *mehte : crefte* in *Jul.* 392 and *henþu : merðu* and *leht : neht* in *Crist* 591–2.

[3] The reading *æht*, adopted by many editors, does not affect the argument here; *æht* in 473 might be held to support *æ* forms, however.

[4] *Anglia* xiii. 11–15.   [5] See Sisam, *Studies* 6.

worthy. Relying, therefore, mainly on the evidence of the Northumbrian genealogy, it would be true to say that the runic signature suggests a date not earlier than the turn of the ninth century.

The conclusions from the linguistic evidence may be summed up as follows; the evidence of the occasional forms in the text suggest a late West Saxon copy of a West Mercian original through an early West Saxon intermediary. The rhymes, which are certainly Anglian, support the theory of a Mercian original, since it can be shown that the name *Cynewulf* makes a Northumbrian original unlikely.

3. THE SOURCE

The poem consists of a narrative followed by a personal epilogue. The theme of the narrative is the Invention of the True Cross, part of the medieval complex of legends about the Holy Cross. Of the four main groups, Inventio Crucis, Origo Crucis, Flagellatio Crucis and Exaltatio Crucis, the Invention legend is probably the oldest. The legends of the Invention and the Exaltation were closely associated with the festivals of the Invention and the Exaltation which, in the Roman church, were celebrated on May 3 and September 14, festivals which account for the frequency of these legends in the medieval Sanctuaria.

It has long been recognized that the source of *Elene* was the *Acta Cyriaci*, a version of which may conveniently be found in the *Acta Sanctorum* for March 4. This legend is probably of eastern origin [1] and combines the story of the finding of the True Cross by St Helena, a legend springing from the discovery of the Holy Sepulchre in 326, with the story of the hostility and ultimate conversion of a Jew called Judas. The development of the Helena legend can be clearly traced in patristic writings of the fourth and fifth centuries, while the history of Judas appears in the writings of the eastern fathers after about the middle of the fifth century.[2] Recensions of the *Acta Cyriaci* are

[1] See Straubinger, *Die Kreuzauffindungslegende.*

[2] For the development of the legend see Tixeront, *Les Origines de l'Église d'Édesse* 163–75.

widespread in Europe during the Middle Ages but the Greek
and Latin versions may be regarded for our purpose as basic,[1]
since it is most probably from them that the western vernacu-
lar versions immediately derive.[2] The Greek and Latin versions
fall into well-defined groups.[3] The Latin texts, for example,
form a group distinct from the Greek and Syriac texts because
they alone have Judas as the brother of St Stephen. St Stephen
Protomartyr could not, in fact, have been the brother of a
Judas living in the time of Constantine, although he could have
been the great-uncle of the traditional Judas Cyriacus, Bishop
of Jerusalem, who suffered martyrdom in 134. Thus the relationship of great-uncle, which appears in most of the Greek and
some of the Syriac versions, may be original [4] and the Latin
version may have arisen, partly from the double reported
speech, and partly from the double genitive in such a phrase
as ὁ ἀδελφὸς τοῦ πατρός μου, which occurs in Vatican MS
Graec. 866.[5] This, however, would imply a homogeneous
development of the Latin versions, since they all have this
relationship.

[1] The earliest versions were probably Syrian and the earliest extant
text known to me is the Syriac text in B.M. MS Add. 14,644 which,
according to Wright's *Catalogue of Syriac MSS in the British Museum*,
is fifth or sixth century. Cp Nestle, *De Sancta Cruce*.

[2] This does not of course imply that the western versions cannot be
indirectly influenced by the eastern versions. An instance of just such
influence seems to be the dating of the Invention festival on May 7
in St Willibrord's Calendar (HBS lv) 29.

[3] For a list of known versions see Holthausen's 4th ed. of *Elene* and
Dubois, *Les Éléments latins dans la Poésie religieuse de Cynewulf*
46–50. To these may be added for Greek: Bodleian MS Arch. Seld.
B. 53, 54b; for Latin: Bodleian MSS Laud Misc. 129, 16b; *ib.* 238, 194;
Fell 4, 208; Canonici Misc. 244, 57; B.M. MSS Royal 7 A. xi, 19; *ib.*
6 A. ii, 1b; Arundel 36, 50b; Egerton 2656, 179; Add. 11,880, 111;
Cmbg. Univ. Lib. MS Mm. 6. 4, 229b. Bodley MS Canonici Graec. 19 ff
190b–197 contains a defective Greek text written probably in the
fifteenth or sixteenth century. Since it is incomplete and late it has
not been collated. Similarly an epitome of the *Acta Cyriaci* in B.M. MS
Arundel 330 is too short to be of any value. Laud Misc. 129 and B.M.
MS Add. 11,880 are more or less contemporary MSS but do not seem
to have been the immediate source.

[4] Cp Ryssel, *Archiv* xciii. 8; Nestle, BZ iv. 336.

[5] See Wotke, *Wiener Studien* xiii. 302–11.

Secondly, the Latin texts never have the September dating of the Invention festival, which is common in texts of eastern origin, where it is probably due to its celebration, in the Nestorian church, on September 13, and in the Syrian church, on September 14. Moreover, the May dating, which properly belongs to the western versions, never appears in the Greek texts, although the date May 10 appears in Lauriotis'[1] text, where, however, it may have been taken from a Latin version.[2]

Thirdly, those Greek and Syriac texts which have Constantine's vision date it from the seventh and not the sixth year of his reign. All the Latin versions, on the other hand, have the sixth year.[3] Comparison of the Latin versions with the Greek and Syriac thus suggests that they developed within a homogeneous tradition, the characteristic features of which are to be found also in *Elene*, which must thus be supposed to have depended upon a version of this type and not, as has sometimes been thought, from a version of the Greek type.

The dependence of Cynewulf on a Latin version is further indicated by the form of the *Hoptasia*, or vision of Constantine, which appears in *Elene*. Whether this motif was an original part of the legend is doubtful. The early Syriac text in MS Add. 14,644, dating from the fifth or sixth century, has no vision. On the other hand, the Rendel Harris codex,[4] from the eighth or ninth century, seems to have had this element, although not certainly as the manuscript is defective at the beginning. That the vision is a later element is further suggested by the appearance, in Greek and Syriac versions, of the *Hoptasia*, without a date, but with a reference to the year of Constantine's reign in which the vision appeared. In these texts the date introduces the Invention narrative. In the Latin versions, on the other hand, the date introduces the vision. This suggests that the *Hoptasia* was a later addition, which, in

[1] See Ἐκκλησιαστικὴ Ἀλήθεια xx. 479–82, 494–6.

[2] No date is given in the abridged MSS B.M. Royal 7 A. xi and Arundel 36 nor in Canonici Misc. 244 and *Legenda Aurea*. Royal 6 A. ii is defective at this point.

[3] Except the defective Egerton MS. The figure is omitted in the abridged Arundel 36 and in the *Legenda Aurea*.

[4] See Nestle, BZ iv. 319–45.

the Latin texts, was welded into the story by the transference of the date to the new beginning of the narrative. The Greek and Syriac versions which have the *Hoptasia* without a date presumably represent an intermediate form. Moreover, the date in the Latin versions, 233,[1] belongs properly to the beginning of the Invention narrative, since it represents the number of years between the burial of the Cross under Trajan and its Invention. The addition of 117, the year of Trajan's death, gives a probable date for the Invention, A.D. 350.[2] The impropriety of the date at the beginning of the *Hoptasia* is emphasized by its conflicting with the dating of the vision in the sixth year of Constantine's reign. It thus appears that *Elene* must derive from a form of the legend in which the vision has not been simply added but incorporated by the transference of the date to the beginning of the text. This again points to a Latin text as the source.

The Latin texts themselves, however, can be grouped according to certain features in the narrative. Thus, the figures 3000 and 1000 which appear in lines 285 and 326 of the poem must be supposed to have been in the source. The number 3000, however, is omitted in Holder's Leiden MS and the motif is absent in Arundel 36 and the *Legenda Aurea*; the figure 1000 is omitted in Royal 7 A. xi and the motif in Arundel 36 and the *Legenda Aurea*. Similarly, the phrase 'two hundred more or less' (El. 634) appears as 233 in the Antwerp MS of ASS., Laud Misc. 238 and Canonici Misc. 244 while it is omitted in Arundel 36. None of these MSS, therefore, represent or derive from the source although they approximate to it in varying degrees.

Other considerations help to eliminate some of the remaining Latin texts. A small group only of these, namely Codex Maximinus of the *Acta Sanctorum* version, Royal 7 A. xi and the St Gall manuscript in Holder's collection,[3] has the baptism of Constantine by Sylvester which appears, also, in *Elene*. Con-

---

[1] Royal 6 A. ii and C.U.L. MS Mm. 6. 4 have 333: B.M. Add. 11,880 223. The figure is omitted in the defective Egerton MS. It is missing in Laud Misc. 238 and the *Legenda Aurea*.

[2] See Nestle, Gött. gel. Anz. 1880. 1530. MS Add. 14,644 has, in fact, 351. Cp *Calendar of St Willibrord* (HBS. lv) 29.

[3] See Holder, *Inventio Sanctae Crucis*.

stantine was, in fact, baptized by Eusebius of Nicomedia [1] and his name appears in many manuscripts. The baptism by Sylvester seems to represent a Roman tradition, although it appears, in two twelfth-century Greek manuscripts, Vatican MS Graec. 2048 and Lauriotis's text, where it may have derived from an earlier Latin version. Secondly, in Elene's second speech, the quotation 'Unto you a son is born' is attributed to Moses in the following Latin texts only: Laud Misc. 129 and 238, Mombritius,[2] Holder's manuscripts b c d, Egerton 2656 and B.M. Add. 11,880. Thus it appears that in a number of respects the St Gall manuscript 225 offers striking parallels with the text of *Elene*. In fact, collation shows that although in a few cases (for example, l. 90 ʒolde ʒeʒlenʒed clearly depends on the reading *litteris aureis* for which St Gall has *litteris*) other texts show closer readings, the St Gall MS may be taken as fairly representing the type of original upon which *Elene* was based.[3] This Latin text, resembling the eighth-century St Gall manuscript in Holder's collection, was perhaps already divided into numbered lections as are the Royal manuscripts. The lections in these two manuscripts correspond fairly closely with each other and with those in *Elene* and may have been traditional. The numbering of the lections in *Elene* can hardly have been the work of the scribe of the Vercelli Book, since they

[1] Eusebius of Nicomedia was an Arian. Hence, perhaps, the substitution of Sylvester, who is connected with Constantine's conversion in Ruffinus and other sources.

[2] Mombritius, *Sanctuarium* (Paris, 1910) i. 376–9.

[3] The St Gall manuscript although probably written at St Gall (see Lowe, *Cod. Lat. Antiq.* vii. 27) could have derived from an English original (cp Levison, *England and the Continent in the Eighth Century* 136 & n.1; 146). Of the ninth-century manuscripts, Add. 11,880 and Laud. Misc. 129, the former is much closer to *Elene* than the latter. Add. 11,880 was probably written at St Emmeram, Regensburg, in the first half of c. 9. It closely resembles St Gall 225 in its readings. See Bischoff, *Die südostdeutschen Schreibschulen* 207. It may be noted here that no source has been found for lines 966–1022 of *Elene* which describe how the queen sends messengers to Rome to report the finding of the cross to Constantine. Since, although the poet elaborates his material, he does not invent episodes except of the most conventional kind we should probably suppose that Cynewulf's original had some warrant for this passage.

occur only in *Elene*. The dating from the Nativity can be paralleled only from a Norse version,[1] which may indicate the existence of a Latin source with this feature, but more probably the coincidence is due simply to the authors' having worked within the same tradition.[2] Finally, it should be noted that attempts have been made to connect *Elene* with an Irish source on the basis of the spellings *Essaias* and *Ceruphin*, which Carlton Brown has shown to be common in manuscripts of Irish provenance.[3] The former occurs also in the Rushworth Gloss and in Lindisfarne, Matt. xiii, 14, and fifteen times in the *Pastoral Care*; the latter, in the form *cheruphim*, in *Andreas* 719 and, in the form *cheruphin*, in the Book of Cerne [4] and in the Canterbury Psalter xvii 11. Against this view it must be objected that the spellings are not necessarily original and, therefore, although they may indicate that the text was at some time copied in a scriptorium with Irish traditions, they cannot be used to show that Cynewulf used a Latin text of Irish provenance. In conclusion, it must be admitted that, with two notable exceptions, there is little in *Elene* which can be shown to be original. The exceptions are, of course, the elaboration in the epic manner of the battle scene and the sea voyage and, secondly, the epilogue.[5] For the rest, a glance at Holthausen's composite text shows that, poetic circumlocution apart, there is little which is not to be found in some version of the *Acta Cyriaci*.

The source of the epilogue may be considered under two headings: the precedent for the use of an epilogue of this kind

---

[1] See *Heilagra Manna Sǫgur*, ed. Unger i. 303–8.

[2] The Nativity dating may, however, be thought to favour an original which does not indicate its method of dating. Most Latin texts date from either the Passion or the Resurrection. Of those texts which have the figure 233 the following, however, have no such indication: Mombritius, Laud Misc. 129, Royal 7 A. xi and Holder a b (St Gall) c.

[3] ESt xl. 1–29; and on less solid grounds *Sachius*.

[4] Ed. Kuypers 85.

[5] There is one notable omission. All the Latin versions mention St Paul's trade. This is omitted in *Elene*. The twelfth-century manuscripts Royal 7A. xi, 6 A. ii and Arundel 36 give an abridged form of the text and omit this detail, but I have found no abridged versions before this period and the omission is no doubt Cynewulf's. Anglo-Saxon translators commonly omit technical details of this kind.

and the source of certain peculiar features in the account of the Day of Judgement. The view that the epilogue is autobiographical and can be related to the vision celebrated in the *Dream of the Rood* can no longer be seriously considered. The epilogue seems to have a twofold inspiration: it is an acknowledgement of the divine gift of poetry, which may have come to the poet, as to Cædmon, in his old age;[1] it is, also, a prayer that God will receive the poem as an acceptable service and a request to the hearer to pray for the poet's soul. There is nothing original either in the dedication of the poem or in the personal tone, and parallels for both these aspects of the epilogue are not far to seek. For example, the more or less contemporary *De Laudibus Sanctae Crucis* [2] of Hrabanus Maurus is dedicated to Christ and the saving power of his Cross, and in dealing with such a theme the poet's thoughts turn naturally to the Day of Judgement.[3] Bede, also, introduced the theme of Judgement with a personal note of the same kind, describing how, solitary and sorrowful, he was oppressed by his own sinfulness and the thought of death.[4] These were sentiments common when Cynewulf wrote, and there is no reason to suppose that the epilogue is autobiographical. Moreover, there is a precedent in Christian literature even for the combination of an epilogue with a narrative, for a personal epilogue following a hagiographical narrative is found in the *Vita Sanctae Mariae Meretricis* of Ephraim of Edessa.[5] Like Cynewulf, Ephraim implies that he is an old man burdened with sin, and he ends with a prayer for mercy at the Judgement. It is not impossible that the addition of such an epilogue to a saint's life was an imitation of Ephraim, since we know that the *Vitae Patrum* were

---

[1] This theme is conventional and appears, also, as is well known, in the Preface to the *Heliand*.

[2] *De Laudibus* II xxviii (P.L. t. cvii col. 294).

[3] The transition from the Invention narrative to meditations on the Last Judgement may have been suggested in part by the liturgy, since the appearance of the Cross at the General Judgement is the theme of versicle and response in the offices for the Invention of the Cross.

[4] *Hymnus de Die Judicii* (P.L. t. xciv cols. 633–8).

[5] *Vitae Patrum* (P.L. t. lxxiii cols. 659–60).

read in Ælfric's day [1] and there is some evidence for a wider knowledge of Ephraim's works in Anglo-Saxon times.[2] In any case, the parallel does at least suggest that the originality of Cynewulf lay less in the conception of an epilogue than in the combination of conventional themes.

The description of the Judgement has been thought to derive from chapter xxi of Alcuin's *De Fide Sanctae et Individuae Trinitatis*. Cook pointed out that *Elene* resembles Alcuin in two respects: the presence of purgatorial fire at the Judgement and the threefold division of mankind into *synfulle, awyrʒede womsceaðan* and *soðfæste*.[3] These characteristics are interesting, since they do not occur in other Old English Judgement scenes. Yet they are not peculiar to Alcuin but, as Carleton Brown has shown,[4] can be paralleled in a number of patristic writings. The threefold division, in particular, has a much closer parallel in Ambrose than in Alcuin, for Ambrose's division into *impii, peccatores, justi* more closely resembles the Old English than Alcuin's *impii, sancti, justi*; Ambrose, moreover, like Cynewulf, describes how the just pass through the fire unscathed. On the other hand, the parallel with Ambrose is not exact, for in *Elene* all rise to judgement, in Ambrose only sinners, since the just rise in the first judgement and the impious, who are judged already, rise to damnation.

4. DATE

Since attempts to identify Cynewulf with an historical figure have been unsuccessful, only internal evidence can be used for dating. The evidence may be summarized in this way: the date of the manuscript puts a terminus in the last half of the tenth century; the linguistic evidence a date not much before the early ninth century. This dating is supported by the order of items in the *Fates*, which seems to represent an order current

---

[1] Cp Aelfric's Latin preface to the *Lives of the Saints*.

[2] Grau thought that the epilogue was based on the Lamentations of Ephraim; see *Studien zur englischen Philologie* xxxi. 15–29. Cp Willard, MLA xlii. 329–30.

[3] *Anglia* xv. 9–20.　　　　　　　　　[4] MLA xviii. 308–34.

only after about 800.[1] If we accept the view that *Elene* was copied in a West Saxon scriptorium during the ninth century, however, the period during which the poem can have been written is greatly reduced. Attempts have been made to place the poem early rather than late on the grounds that in the eighth century the cult of the cross was particularly popular in England. But although the Invention festival seems to have been of Gallican provenance and does not appear, as is well known, in the Gregorian Sacramentary there is no evidence either that the cult of the Cross in general ceased after the eighth century or that the Invention festival was not known in England later in the Anglo-Saxon period. On the contrary manuscripts such as the Leofric Missal, MS C.C.C.C. 270 and the Missal of Robert of Jumièges have proper masses for the feast and both Aelfric's account of the *Adoratio Crucis* [2] and the *Regularis Concordia* testify to the popularity of the cult. We hear of relics of the True Cross being presented to King Alfred in the ninth century [3] and of a Frankish mission in the tenth presenting to King Athelstan a magnificent gift consisting of relics associated with Constantine and the True Cross.[4] In favour of a ninth-century date it may, also, be pointed out that the acrostic was a most popular pastime among Carolingian scholars as the poetry of the period testifies.[5] At such a time Cynewulf would have been in the height of the poetic fashion in signing his poems in this way. Runes too were probably a fashionable study at this period.[6] The evidence, in fact, plainly suggests that Cynewulf was a West Mercian poet writing in the first half of the ninth century.

[1] Sisam, *Studies* 9.

[2] *Pastoral Letters*, ed. Fehr 161–4. Cp Brieger, *Medieval Studies* iv. 85–96.

[3] ASC. MS E 883; cp Stevens, *Yale Studies in English* 23.

[4] William of Malmesbury, *Gesta Regum* (RS) i. 150–1.

[5] Cp *Poetae Latini Aevi Carolini* (MGH, Poetarum Latinorum Medii Aevi 1–4) *passim*.

[6] Cp Derolez, *Runica Manuscripta* 217.

THE TEXT

The punctuation and use of capitals is modern and the text is printed in lines in the modern fashion. Square brackets have been used to indicate editorial additions. MS abbreviations and suspensions have been expanded without comment. The abbreviations and suspensions expanded are the tilde which is used for *m* and for *ne* in *þōn*, *þ̄*, roman figures for numerals, *ʒ̄* for *ʒeard* in 16, 774 and for *ʒe* in 1311, *ꞇswēr* for *andsweredon* in 396, *sēs* in 504, the w-rune for *wyn* in 788, *kt* for *kalend* in 1228. 7 is used as an abbreviation for the first syllable of *andsware* 166, 318, 375, 456, 462, 545, 619, 642, 662; *andwlitan* 298; *andsec* 472; *andweardlice* 1140.

CYNEWULF'S ELENE

ÞA pæs aȝanȝen   ȝeara hpyrftum
tu hund 7 þreo   ȝeteled rimes
spylce þrittiȝ eac   þinȝȝemearces
pintra for porulde   þæs þe pealdend Ȝod
5 acenned pearð   cyninȝa puldor
in middanȝeard   þurh mennisc heo
soðfæstra leoht;   þa pæs syxte ȝéar
Constantines   caserdomes
þæt he Rompara   in rice pearð
10 ahæfen hildfruma   to hereteman.
Ðæs se leodhpata   lindȝeborȝa
eorlum arfæst,   æðel[i]nȝes peox
rice under roderum;   he pæs riht cyninȝ,
ȝuðpearð ȝumena.   Hine Ȝod trymede

TEXTUAL VARIANTS: (8) *Constantines*] Maier (prius ... *nus*). (12)
æðelinȝes] *æðelnȝes*.

---

(1) pæs: cp *Jul.* 678; *El.* 284–5; the singular may be due to the inversion or to the collective numeral. Cp Bauch, *Die Kongruenz in dev ags.
Poesie* 52.

(2b) 'reckoning in numbers'. Cp *Phoenix* 29; *Genesis* 1335–6; *Andreas*
1035.

(3b) Cp *Andreas* 148. BT suggest 'measuring of time by events' but
the meaning is perhaps 'period of time'. *þinȝ* is cognate with Gothic
þeihs and the meaning 'time' is probably preserved here and in *þinȝ*
'assembly called at regular intervals'. See Hoops, *Reallexicon* s.v. *Ding*.

(11) Grein, *Bibliothek*, suggested *lindhpata* for *leodhpata* but emendation is perhaps unnecessary. *Leod-* may represent a fusion of the
variants *leoþu-/liþ-* with confusion between *ð* and *d* as elsewhere in the
manuscript (cp note to 522). Or *leod-* is possibly intensive; cp *reȝnþeof,
reȝnheard, dryhtenbealo, ðeodfeond*, although the latter, which occurs in
Wulfstan, may be due to ON *þjóð-*; cp Kock, ESt xliv. 393. Grein
suggests *leodȝeborȝa* for *lindȝeborȝa*; Holthausen, *Cynewulfs Elene*
(1910) *leodȝebyrȝa* after *El.* 203, 556; *Beo.* 269. But weak nouns derived
from verbal stems have mutation only if they are *-jan* stems and the
form in the text may represent a genuine unmutated variant. The word
means 'shield protector'. Cp *Germania* § 6.

15 mærðum 7 mihtum   þæt he maneȝum pearð
   ȝeond middanȝeard   mannum to hroðer
   perþeodum to præce   syððan þæpen ahóf
   þið hetendum.   Him þæs hild boden,
   piȝes poma;   perod samnodan
20 Huna leode   7 Hreðȝotan,
   foron fyrdhpate Francan 7 Hu[ȝ]as,
   pæron hpate peras
   ȝearpe to ȝuðe;   ȝaras lixtan
   priðene pælhlencan,   pordum 7 bordum

(21a) The *n* of *foron* seems to have been added later and a point inserted to separate *foron* and *fyrd*. (21b) *Huȝas*] *hunas*.

(17a) Cp *Beo.* 5. The functions of the good king are the consolation of the people and the confusion of their foes. Ekwall's reading *wra/æþe* (Anglia Beibl xxxiii. 65) is unnecessary.

(19a) Cp *El.* 71 'spefnes poma'. Etymologically *poma* is a sound or noise as in the cognate Lat. *vox* and OE 'pom 7 pop' in *Cr. & Sat.* 332. A secondary meaning 'noise of storm or battle' seems to occur here, in *Wand.* 103 and in ON *ómi* a *heiti* of Odin, god of storm and battle; and, perhaps, in *Ex.* 100; *Jul.* 136, 663. The meaning 'harbinger', 'one who speaks', is suggested by the cognate verb *peman* and by *dæg(red)poma* for the rising sun, or harbinger of day in *Guth.* 1218, 1292; *Andreas* 125. This sense is probably to be understood for 'spefnes poma' in *Dan.* 118, 538; *El.* 71. The phrase may derive from the medieval view of dreams as divine manifestations. Translate 'revelation of a dream'. Cp Schücking, *Untersuchungen zur Bedeutungslehre der ags. Dichtersprache* 91–8.

(20) For the Hreþgoths see Gradon MLR xlii. 161–72.

(21) The emendation *Huȝas*, first suggested by Zupitza, is supported by the association of these people with the Franks in heroic poetry. Cp *Beo.* 2910 ff.

(22) Klaeber, *Anglia* xxix. 271 'spylce Hetpare; pæron hpate peras'. For the Hetpare in association with the Hugas and the Franks cp *Beo.* But the half-line is complete in both metre and sense and, moreover, alliterates with the previous line. It may, therefore, be a metrical variant. Cp 371, 439, 451, 518, 582, 614, 1277.

(24b) Perhaps a corruption of 'ordum and bordum'. But the reference may be to some ceremony connected with the raising of the standard; cp *Ex.* 566–7. The clashing of weapons was a sign of assent (cp Tacitus, *Hist.* V xvii; *Germania* § 11) and it may have had other ceremonial uses: and the banners were sacred as representing images of sacred beasts and symbols of the gods. Cp Tacitus, *Hist.* IV xxii; *Germania* ed. Anderson 69–70. For ritual observances before battle see Amm. Marcell. xxxi. 7, 10.

25 hofon herecombol;   þa pæron heardinӡas
   speotole ӡesamnod   7 eal [syb] ӡeador.
   Fór folca ӡedryht,   fyrdleoð aӡól
   pulf on pealde,   pælrune ne mað;
   uriӡfeðera   earn sanӡ ahóf
30 laðum on laste;   lunӡre scynde
   ofer burӡen[de]   beaduþreata mæst
   herӡum to hilde   spylce Huna cyninӡ
   ymbsittendra   aþer meahte
   abannan to beadpe   burӡpiӡendra.
35 Fór fyrda mæst,   feðan trymedon,
   eoredcestum   þæt on ælfylce
   deareðlacende   on Danubie,
   stærcedfyrhðe   stæðe picedon
   ymb þæs pæteres pylm   þerodes breahtme.
40 Þoldon Rómpara   rice ӡeþrinӡan
   herӡum áhyðan;   þær þearð Huna cyme
   cuð ceasterparum;   þa se casere heht

(26) *syb* not in the MS. (31) *burgende*] *burgenta*. (35) Maier notes
three or four letters erased after *fór*. Now only a large stain is visible.

(26b) For the emendation see Sievers, Gött. gel. Anz. (1882) 997;
Grimm read 'eal speot ӡeador'. Perhaps a tribal name such as Spæfe or
Seaxe has been lost.

(31a) Early editors assumed a connection with *ent* 'giant'. Thus
Grimm read *burg enta*. Arngart, *English Studies* xxvii. 20–1, suggests
that the barbarians are gathering in an old castle. Grimm suggested
as an alternative *Burgendas* or *Burgendan* (Grein *Burgenta*) and this
view has been supported by Grattan, in MLR xv. 178, where he points
out that the Burgundians were near the Danube in the third century.
Objections to this are, firstly, that *Burgenda* would be the normal form;
but *t* and *d* are similar and the manuscript reading might exemplify a
common error, the substitution of a common for a proper noun as
perhaps in *Beo.* 1960, 1145; secondly, the function of *ofer* is then obscure
unless it is a noun and 'ofer Burgenda' means 'the banks of the Danube'.
But the intransitive *scynde* and the D half-line with alliteration on the
second lift tell against this. The text assumes *burgende* 'city boundary'.
For *ende* 'edge' see *Dream of the Rood* 29; *El.* 59.

(35–6a) 'the greatest of armies advanced—fell into formation—in
hosts'. The phrase 'getrym(m)ed feþa' glosses *cuneus*; see Wright-
Wülcker 216, 11–12; 110, 35.

onȝean ȝramum   ȝuðȝelæcan
under earhfære   ofstum myclum
45 bannan to beadþe,   beran ut þræce
rincas under roderum.   Þæron Rompare,
secȝas siȝeRófe   sona ȝeȝearpod
pæpnum to piȝȝe   þeah hie perod læsse
hæfdon to hilde   þone Huna cininȝ.   fol. 121ᵇ
50 Ridon ymb rófne,   þonne rand dynede,
camppudu clynede,   cyninȝ þreate fór
herȝe to hilde,   hrefen uppe ȝól
pan 7 pǽlfel.   Þerod pæs on tyhte;
hleopon hornboran,   hreopan friccan,
55 mearh moldan træd,   mæȝen samnode
cafe to cease.   Cyninȝ pæs áfyrhted,
eȝsan ȝeaclad   siððan elþeodiȝe
Huna 7 Hreða   here sceapedon
ðæt he on Rompara   rices ende

(45) *beran ut:* probably intransitive. Cp ON *bera út*; *Andreas* 1221 and Kock, Lunds Universitets *Aarsskrift* (N.F. Pt. i) xviii. 22–3.

(50b–51a) For rhyme see Lefèvre, *Anglia* vi. 181–240; Kluge, PBB ix. 422–50.

(56–61) There are two difficulties here: 1. *sceapedon* in 58 does not agree with its apparent subject *cyninȝ*; 2. the MS reading 'ðæt he... samnode' implies that the antecedent of *he* is Constantine, which makes poor sense. *Sceapedon* has been explained as referring to both the king and the army (Körner, *Einleitung in das Studium d. Ags.* 269); to the scribe's having taken *elþeodiȝe* as the subject, as Holthausen (*Elene* 1936); or as due to a change of number (Klaeber, MPh iii. 449); or it has been emended to *sceapede* (cp ten Brink, AfdA v. 58). The latter may be supported by the Latin reading 'Videns... quia multitudo erat innumerabilis contristatus est ualde et timuit usque ad mortem'. But more probably *sceapedon* is intransitive. Cp Körner, *op.cit.* This use is not recorded but *seon* 'appear' occurs in Byrhtferth's Manual, ed. Crawford (EETS 177) 86, 8. *He* in 59 could refer to the Hunnish king, as Pogatscher suggested in *Anglia* xxiii. 289–90; or to *here* as suggested by Kock in ESt xliv. 394; or could be omitted as by Schaar in *Studia Neophilologica* xix. 312–13; Klaeber (ESt lv. 283) suggests that *samnode* is intransitive. But more probably *he* is plural (see p. 13) and the singular verb is due to scribal confusion. Thus read *samnodon* with ten Brink, *op.cit.* 58, and translate 'the king was fearful...when the barbarians...appeared because they had collected an army etc'.

(57) *egsan:* 'very'; see Schücking, *op.cit.* 35.

60 ymb þæs pæteres stæð   perod samnod[on]
mæȝen unríme. Módsorȝe pæȝ
Rómpara cyninȝ, rices ne pende
for perodleste, hæfde piȝena to lyt
eaxlȝestealna pið ofermæȝene
65 hrora to hilde; here picode
eorlas ymb æðelinȝ eȝstreame neah
on neapeste nihtlanȝne fyrst
þæs þe he feonda ȝefær fyrmest ȝesæȝon.
Þa pearð on slæpe sylfum ætyped,
70 þam casere þær he on corðre spæf,
siȝerofum ȝeseȝen spefnes poma.
Þuhte him plitescyne on peres hade
hpit 7 hipbeorht hæleða nathpylc
ȝeyped ænlicra þonne he ær oððe sið
75 ȝeseȝe under speȝle. He of slæpe onbræȝd
eofurcumble beþeaht; him se ár hraðe,
plitiȝ puldres boda pið þinȝode
7 be naman nemde— nihthelm toȝlad—
'Constantinus, heht þe cyninȝ enȝla
80 pyrda pealdend, þære beodan
duȝuða dryhten; ne ondræd þu ðe
ðeah þe elþeodiȝe eȝesan hpopan
heardre hilde; þu to heofenum beseoh
on puldres peard; þær ðu praðe findest
85 siȝores tacen'. He þæs sona ȝearu
þurh þæs halȝan hæs— hreðerlocan onspeon—
up locade spa him se ár ábead,

---

(60) *samnodon*] *samnode*. (61) Maier read *moðsorȝe*. (69) The *p* in *ætyped* has been altered from a *þ*.   (85–6) A point separates *ȝearu* and *þurh*. (87) A tag is used to separate *se* and *ár*.

(65–75) Note the use of linked alliteration.
(71) See 19a.
(82) *hpopan* is subj.; cp *ȝecyðan* 409; *piston* 459; *ahenȝon* 475.
(86b) *Jul.* 79 suggests the translation 'he spoke'. See Ekwall, Anglia Beibl xxxiii. 65. The subject of *onspeon* is probably to be understood from *halgan* (cp *Anglia* xxiii. 280). In *Crist* 1055 *hreðerloca* is the part of the body containing the thoughts. Cp *Elene* 1249.

fæle friðopebba;   ʒeseah he frætpum beorht
pliti puldres treo   ofer polcna hróf
90 ʒolde ʒe[ʒ]lenʒed;   ʒimmas lixtan;
pæs se blaca béam   bocstafum apriten
beorhte 7 leohte,   'Mid þys beacne ðu
on þam frecnan fære   feond oferswiðesð,
ʒeletest lað perod';   þa þæt leoht ʒepát,
95 up siðode   7 se ar somed
on clænra ʒemanʒ;   cyninʒ pæs þy bliðra
7 þe sorʒleasra,   secʒa aldor   fol. 122ᵃ
on fyrhðsefan   þurh þa fæʒeran ʒesyhð:—

.ii.

HEHT þa onlice   æðelinʒa hleo,
100 beorna beaʒʒifa   spa he þæt beacen ʒeseah,
heria hildfruma,   þæt him on heofonum ær
ʒeieped pearð,   ofstum myclum
Constantinus   Cristes róde,
tíreadiʒ cyninʒ,   tacen ʒepyrcan.
105 Heht þa on uhtan   mid ærdæʒe
piʒend preccan   7 pæpenþræce,
hebban heorucumbul   7 þæt haliʒe treo
him beforan ferian   on feonda ʒemanʒ,
beran beacen Ꜧodes.   Býman sunʒon
110 hlude for herʒum,   hrefn peorces ʒefeah,
uriʒfeðra   earn sið beheold
pælhreopra piʒ;   pulf sanʒ áhof,
holtes ʒehleða;   hildeʒesa stod.
Þær pæs borda ʒebrec   7 beorna ʒeþrec,
115 heard handʒespinʒ   7 herʒa ʒrinʒ
syððan heo earhfære   ærest metton;

(90) ʒeʒlenʒed] ʒelenʒed. (91) Two letters have been erased before
apriten. (97) The last two letters of sorʒleasra on an erasure.

(106) 'arouse the warriors and hostility'. Zeugma.
(114) Compound subjects can take a singular or plural verb. But the
singular verb here may be due to the inversion. Cp *El.* 751, 892; Bauch,
op.cit. 60–2.

on þæt fæӡe folc   flana scuras,
ӡaras ofer ӡeolorand   on ӡramra ӡemanӡ,
hetend heor[u]ӡrimme   hildenædran
120 þurh finӡra ӡepeald forð onsendan.
Stopon stiðhidiӡe,   stundum præcon,
bræcon bordhreðan;   bil in dufan,
þrunӡon þræchearde;   þa þæs þuf hafen,
seӡn for speot[u]m,   siӡeleoð ӡalen;
125 ӡylden ӡrima,   ӡaras lixtan
on her[e]felda;   hæðene ӡrunӡon,
feollon friðelease,   fluӡon instæpes
Huna leode   spa þæt haliӡe treo
aræran heht   Rompara cyninӡ
130 heaðofremmende.   Þurdon heardinӡas
pide toprecene;   sume piӡ fornam,
sume unsofte aldor ӡeneredon
on þam heresiðe,   sume healfcpice
fluӡon on fæsten   7 féore burӡon
135 æfter stanclifum,   stede peardedon

(119) *heoruӡrimme*] *heora ӡrimme.* (124) *speotum*] *speotolū.* (126)
herefelda] *hera felda.*

---

(122) bordhreðan: cp *scyldhreoða. Sceldhreða* and *scyldreða* gloss
testudo and since *Exodus* 113 and 159 suggest that *bordhreða* and
scyldhreða were interchangeable terms, presumably *bordhreða* can have
this sense also, although it is usually glossed as *clýpei tegmen.* *-hreða*
is probably to be connected with *hreða* 'garment' and etymologically
bordhreða seems to mean 'shield covering' [cp *bordðeaca*] from which
it may be possible to assume a divergent development to *clýpei tegmen*
and *testudo.* Either sense would be possible here.

(124a) The MS reading is probably due, as Grein-Wülcker suggest,
to a blending of *speotum* and *speotole.* But *speotolum* might be a variant
of *speotole* as *miclum : micle. For* would then be a verb and the phrase
parenthetic.

(124b) Cp *'Carmen triumphale .i. imperiale* siӡarlic leoþ' in Napier,
Anecdota Oxoniensia (Mod. & Med. Series) 4 xi; 36, 1347. The etymo-
logical sense of *siӡe* 'magic', which is preserved in ME *siӡaldrie, siӡӡal-
dren,* is probably not intended here. *Ʒalan,* originally 'sing a spell', is
here best translated 'chant'. For the semantic association between
'cry' and 'charm' cp ModE 'charm'.

(134) fæsten: 'place of safety'. Cp *Maldon* 194.

(135) æfter: 'along'. Cp Norw. *etter,* dial. *after.*

ymb Danubie,   sume drenc fornam
on laʒostreame   lifes æt ende.
Ða pæs modiʒra   mæʒen on luste,
ehton elþeoda   oð þæt æfen forð
140 fram dæʒes orde;   daroðæs fluʒon,
hildenædran,   heap pæs ʒescyrded
laðra lindþered,   lýthpon becpom
Huna herʒes   ham eft þanon.
þa pæs ʒesyne   þæt siʒe forʒeaf
145 Constantino   cyninʒ ælmihtiʒ   fol. 122ᵇ
æt þam dæʒpeorce,   dompeorðunʒa,
rice under roderum   þurh his rode treo.
Gepat þa heriʒa helm   ham eft þanon
huðe hremiʒ—hild pæs ʒesceaden—
150 piʒʒe ʒepeorðod.   Com þa piʒena hleo
þeʒna þreate   þryðbord stenan,

(140) daroðæs] daroð/æsc.

(138–9) mæʒen...ehton: note false concord. The number of collective nouns is variable in OE; cp 231, 283, 762; Bauch, op.cit. 33–51.

(140b) daroðæs: if the MS reading is kept it represents either a compound noun as suggested by most editors and Klaeber, *Archiv* cxiii. 147–8; but *æsc* is masc. and cannot, therefore, properly be the subject of *flugon*; or asyndeton as Holthausen, Anglia Beibl. xv. 73–4 (cp Swaen, *Anglia* xvii. 124). Two consecutive nouns without a conjunction appear in Beo. 398, 1157, 1224, 1259 etc: but such collocations usually form a half-line. The reading in the text is Zupitza's *daroðas* with what may be a late spelling. But the scansion is irregular and the reading *daroð*, *æsc* is perhaps to be preferred.

(141) For *ʒescyrded* see AEW s.v. *scierdan*. Emendation is unnecessary.

(150–2) Cp *Beo.* 123–5.

(151b) There is no satisfactory solution of this crux. Körner (ESt ii. 254–5) tentatively equated *stenan* with NE stain and drew attention to a reference to coloured shields in *Germania* § 6. But apart from the contextual awkwardness there is no proof that *stænan* has a meaning other than 'to stone'. The meaning 'to adorn with jewels' assumed by some critics belongs properly to *astænan*. Moreover, although the Sutton Hoo shield and perhaps the obscure *staimbort* in *Hildebrandslied* 65 might be cited as evidencing jewelled shields, the phrase as a whole is still inexplicable. The identification with *stenan* 'to groan', 'to crash' first suggested by Körner is also contextually difficult. Sarrazin (ZfdPh xxxii. 548–9) emended to *þryðbold secan*. Perhaps we should beadURÓf cyninȝ   burȝa neosan.

Heht þa piȝena peard   þa pisestan

snude to sionoðe   þa þe snyttro cræft

155 þurh fyrnȝeprito   ȝefriȝen hæfdon,

heoldon hiȝeþancum   hæleða rædas.

Ða þæs fricȝȝan onȝan   folces aldor,

siȝerof cyninȝ   ofer sid peorod,

pære þær æniȝ   yldra oððe ȝinȝra

160 þe him to soðe   secȝȝan meahte

ȝaldrum cyðan   hpæt se ȝod þære,

boldes brytta,   'þe þis his beacen pæs,

þe me spa leoht oðypde   7 mine leode ȝenerede,

tacna torhtost   7 me tír forȝeaf,

165 piȝsped pið praðum   þurh þæt plitiȝe treo'.

Hio him andspare   æniȝe ne meahton

aȝifan toȝenes   ne ful ȝeare cuðon

speotole ȝesecȝȝan   be þam siȝebeacne;

þa þa pisestan   pordum cpædon

170 for þam heremæȝene   þæt hit heofoncyninȝes

tacen pære   7 þæs tpeo nære;

þa þæt ȝefruȝnon   þa þurh fulpihte

(169) The last two letters of *cpædon* appear to be on an erasure.

---

read *ste(o)ran* (cp BT) and take *þryðbord* as 'mighty ship'. The confusion of *n* and *r* is not uncommon. The ineptitude of the phrase in the context is not without parallel in the poem.

(161b) Idiomatic use of *hpæt* with a masculine predicate. Cp 905 where *þis* is used with a feminine predicate. Cp Bauch, *op.cit.* 28–9.

(162a) 'lord of the palace'? Cp *boldaȝend*. *Bold* was probably an important building. It is used for the king's residence in Bede (ed. Miller (EETS 95) 140, 22–5) and in a phrase indicating princely power in *Beo.* 2195–6. Cp OE *heafodbotl* which translates Lat. *manerium*. Its frequency as an element in place names may, also, indicate a building of importance. Cp Ekwall, *Dictionary of English Place Names* s.v. *bōþl*. Zupitza suggested emending to *blædes brytta*, Körner to *ȝoldes brytta*. If the phrase is retained it should, perhaps, be taken as paralled to *siȝerof cyninȝ* in 158.

(172–6) The Latin *Audientes autem hoc pauci Christiani laeti* etc supports the translation 'when those who had been baptized heard that, though they were few, their hearts were glad and their spirits rejoiced that they might make known to the emperor the grace of the gospel'.

lærde pæron, him pæs leoht sefa,
ferhð ʒefeonde, þeah hira fea pæron,
175 ðæt hie for þam casere cyðan moston
ʒodspelles ʒife, hu se ʒasta helm
in þrynesse þrymme ʒepeorðad
acenned pearð, cyninʒa puldor,
7 hu on ʒalʒan pearð Ʒodes aʒen bearn
180 áhanʒen for herʒum heardum pitum.
Alysde leoda bearn of locan deofla,
ʒeomre ʒastas 7 him ʒife sealde
þurh þa ilcan ʒesceaft þe him ʒeyped pearð
sylfum on ʒesyhðe, siʒores tacne,
185 pið þeoda þræce 7 hu ðy þriddan dæʒe
of byrʒenne beorna puldor
of deaðe áras, dryhten ealra
hæleða cynnes 7 to heofonum ástah.
Ðus ʒleaplice ʒastʒerynum
190 sæʒdon siʒerofum spa fram Siluestre
lærde pæron; æt þam se leodfruma
fulpihte onfenʒ 7 þæt forð ʒeheold
on his daʒana tíd dryhtne to pillan:—

.iii.

ÐA pæs on sælum sinces brytta,   fol. 123ª
195 niðheard cyninʒ; pæs him nipe ʒefea
befolen in fyrhðe; pæs him frofra mæst
7 hyht[a][h]ihst heofonrices peard;

(186) The first three letters of *beorna* appear to be on an erasure.
(197) *hyhta hihst*] hyht nihst. (199) An *e* seems to have been erased
after *cyðan*.

(184a) 'before his very eyes'.
(184b) 'by the token of victory'. The phrase is parallel to 183a. For
the interchange of an instrumental with a prepositional phrase see
Kock, ESt xliv. 394–5; Körner, ESt ii. 255. For the epithet see Patch,
MLA xxxiv. 233–57.
(193) The unusual form *daʒana* may be a mistake but there is some
evidence of weak forms of *dæʒ*; see BT, BTS *dæʒ*, Sievers, *Anglia* i. 577.
(197a) Emendations to *hyhta hihst* are on the analogy of *Guthlac* 63.

34

onȝan þa dryhtnes æ   dæȝes 7 nihtes
þurh Ȝastes ȝife   ȝeorne cyðan
200 7 hine soðlice   sylfne ȝetenȝde,
ȝoldpine ȝumena,   in Ȝodes þeopdom
æscróf, unslap. Þa se æðelinȝ fand,
leodȝebyrȝa,   þurh larsmiðas,
ȝuðheard, ȝarþrist   on Ȝodes bocum
205 hpær ahanȝen pæs   heriȝes beorhtme
on rode treo   rodora paldend
æfstum þurh inpit   spa se ealda feond
forlærde liȝesearpum,   leode fortyhte,
Iudea cyn   þæt hie Ȝod sylfne
210 ahenȝon herȝa fruman;   þæs hie in hynðum sculon
to pidan feore   perȝðu dreoȝan.
þa pæs Cristes lóf   þam casere
on firhðsefan   forð ȝemyndiȝ
ymb þæt mære treo   7 þa his modor het
215 feran foldpeȝe   folca þreate
to Iudeum,   ȝeorne secan
piȝena þreate   hpær se puldres beam
haliȝ under hrusan   hyded pære,
æðelcyninȝes ród;   Elene ne polde
220 þæs siðfates   sæne peorðan
ne ðæs pilȝifan   pord ȝehyrpan,
hiere sylfre suna   ac pæs sona ȝearu,

(202) *æscrof* seems to be on an erasure.
(204) The last two letters of *ȝarþrist* appear to be on an erasure.
(221) *p* of *ȝehyrpan* above the line and a tag. (222) The *o* of *sona* appears to be on an erasure. The *p* of *pæs* has been added in the margin.

(205) It is not clear whether *beorhtm* should be regarded as a variant of *bearhtm*, *breahtm* (OE *brecan*; Corpus Gloss *braechtme*; Epinal *brectme*; OS *brahtum*). It is not usually recognized as such in the grammars. It may be an analogical reformation with the *e*-grade or due to confusion with *beorhtm*.

(212–14) Since *ȝemyndiȝ* with dative usually means 'memorable to' or 'worthy of remembrance by' we might here expect *ȝemyndiȝ* with a genitive, 'mindful of'. The translation, however, is probably 'Then was Christ's glory thenceforth present to the emperor's mind, concerning the Holy Tree...'; but Pogatscher (*Anglia* xxiii. 289) suggests that *pæs* is common to *casere* and *ȝemyndiȝ* which is possible.

    ƿif on ƿillsið   spa hire þeoruda helm,
    byrnpiȝȝendra,   beboden hæfde.
225 Onȝan þa ofstlice   eorla menȝu
    to flote fysan;   fearoðhenȝestas
    ymb ȝeofenes stæð   ȝearpe stodon,
    sælde sæmearas   sunde ȝetenȝe.
    Ða þæs orcnæpe   idese siðfæt
230 siððan þæȝes helm   perode ȝesohte;
    þær planc maniȝ   æt pendelsæ
    on stæðe stodon.   Stundum præcon
    ofer mearcpaðu   mæȝen æfter oðrum
    7 þa ȝehlodon   hildesercum,
235 bordum 7 ordum,   byrnpiȝendum,
    perum 7 pifum,   pæȝhenȝestas.
    Leton þa ofer fifelpæȝ   famiȝe scriðan
    bronte brimþisan,   bord oft onfenȝ
    ofer earhȝeblond   yða spenȝas.
240 Sæ spinsade.   Ne hyrde ic sið ne ær   fol. 123^b
    on eȝstreame   idese lædan,
    on merestræte   mæȝen fæȝ[e]rre.
    Þær meahte ȝesion   se ðone sið beheold
    brecan ofer bæðpeȝ,   brimpudu snyrȝan,
245 under s[p]ellinȝum   samearh plæȝean,
    padan pæȝflotan.   piȝan pæron bliðe
    collenferhðe,   cpen siðes ȝefeah
    syþþan to hyðe   hrinȝedstefnan
    ofer laȝofæsten   ȝeliden hæfdon
250 on Creca land;   ceolas leton
    æt sæfearoðe   sande beprecene,

---

(237) *Leton* on an erasure; *famiȝe* was written first with *æ* the second
stroke of which has been erased. (239) The last two letters of *spenȝas*
seem to be on an erasure. (242) *fæȝerre*] *fæȝrre*. (245) *spellinȝum*]
spellinȝum.

(230a) pæges helm: cp Riddle lxxvii. 1; Exeter Gnomes 73.
(245a) spellinȝ: 'swelling sail'. Although a *hapax legomenon*, this,
Thorpe's reading, is perhaps possible.,
(245b) Cp Chaucer *shippes hoppestres*.
(251b) 'lashed with sand'. The emendation to *sunde*, supported by
Andreas 424, gives better sense. The suggestion is from Grein.

ald yð[h]ofu　oncrum fæste
on brime bidan　beorna ʒeþinʒes
hpone heo sio ʒuðcpen　ʒumena þreate
255　ofer eastpeʒas　eft ʒesohte.
Ðær pæs on eorle　eðʒesyne
broʒden byrne　7 bill ʒecost,
ʒeatolic ʒuðscrud,　ʒrimhelm maniʒ,
ænlic eoforcumbul.　Þæron æscpiʒan,
260　secʒʒas ymb siʒecpen　siðes ʒefysde;
fyrdrincas frome　foron on luste
on Creca land,　caseras bodan,
hilderincas　hyrstum ʒeperede.
Þær pæs ʒesyne　sincʒim locen
265　on þam hereþreate,　hlafordes ʒifu.
Þæs seo eadhreðiʒe　Elene ʒemyndiʒ,
þriste on ʒeþance　þeodnes pillan,
ʒeorn on mode　þæt hio Iudeas
ofer herefeldas　heape ʒecoste,
270　lindpiʒendra　land ʒesohte,
secʒa þreate.　Spa hit siððan ʒelamp
ymb lytel fæc　þæt ðæt leodmæʒen,
ʒuðrofe hæleþ　to Hierusalem
cpomon in þa ceastre　corðra mæste,
275　eorlas æscrófe　mid þa æðelan cpen:—:　iiii.

HEHt ða ʒebeodan　burʒsittendum,
þam snoterestum　side 7 pide,
ʒeond Iudeas　ʒumena ʒehpylcum,
meðelheʒende　on ʒemot cuman

(252) yðhofu] yð liofu. (253) Maier bidan [prius bidam]. (279) meðel
heʒende] meðel/henʒende.

---

(252) Arngart, op.cit. 19 suggests yðliodu; cp leoþu Rhyming Poem 14.
But the traditional emendation to yðhofu 'ship', suggested by Gen. 1316,
is palaeographically more convincing.
(256-9) Cp Beo. 303-6, 1243-6.
(279) meðelheʒende: or herʒende? cp BT. Confusion of r and n is not
uncommon in MSS. But the reading meðelheʒende, adopted by most
editors, is credible on the supposition that the scribe anticipated the

280 þa ðe deoplicost   dryhtnes ȝeryno
     þurh rihte æ   reccan cuðon.
     Ða þæs ȝesamnod   of sidþeȝum
     mæȝen unlytel   þa ðe Moyses æ
     reccan cuðon.   Þær on rime þæs
285 þreo þusendo   þæra leoda
     alesen to lare.   Onȝan þa leoflic þif
     þeras Ebrea   þordum neȝan,
     'Ic þæt ȝearolice   onȝiten hæbbe
     þurȝ þitȝena   þordȝeryno
290 on Ȝodes bocum   þæt ȝe ȝeardaȝum   fol. 124ᵃ
     þyrðe þæron   þuldorcyninȝe,
     dryhtne dyre   7 dædhþæte.
     Hþæt ȝe þære snyttro   unþíslice,
     praðe þiðþeorpon   þa ȝe perȝdon þane
295 þe eop of perȝðe   þurh his þuldre[s] miht,
     fram liȝcpale   lysan þohte,
     of hæftnede.   Ȝe mid horu speopdon
     on þæs andplitan   þe eop eaȝena leoht
     fram blindnesse   bote ȝefremede,
300 edniopunȝa   þurh þæt æðele spald
     7 fram unclænum   oft ȝenerede
     deofla ȝastum.   Ȝe deaþe þone
     deman onȝunnon   se ðe of deaðe sylf
     þoruld apehte   on þera corþre
305 in þæt ærre líf   eopres cynnes.
     Spa ȝe modblinde   menȝan onȝunnon
     liȝe þið soðe,   leoht wið þystrum,
     æfst þið are,   inþitþancum
     proht þebbedan;   eop seo perȝðu forðan
310 sceðþeð scyldfullum.   Ȝe þa sciran miht

(295) *þuldres*] þuldre.   (310) *scran* with *i* above the line and a tag.

---

participial ending. The lack of concord may be due to predicative use;
cp 992 and *JJJ* 19–21.
   (293) The alliteration is probably *hp*: *p*; cp *Guth.* 263. The emendation
to *ealre* (or *ealle*) *snyttro*, first suggested by ten Brink, *op.cit* .59, is thus
not essential although supported by the Latin 'omnem sapientiam'.

deman onȝunnon, on ȝedþeolan lifdon
þeostrum ȝeþancum oð þysne dæȝ.
Ȝanȝaþ nú snude, snyttro ȝeþencaþ
peras pisfæste, pordes cræftiȝe,
315 þa ðe eopre ǽ, æðelum cræftiȝe,
on ferhðsefan fyrmest hæbben
þa me soðlice secȝan cunnon,
andspare cyðan for eop[ic] forð
tacna ȝehpylces þe ic him to sece.'
320 Eodan þa on ȝerum reoniȝmode,
eorlas æcleaþe eȝesan ȝeþreade,
ȝehðum ȝeomre eorne sohton
þa pisestan pordȝeryno
þæt hio þære cpene oncpeðan meahton
325 spa tiles spa traȝes spa hio him to sohte.
Hio þa on þreate þusendo manna
fundon ferhðȝleapra þa þe fyrnȝemynd
mid Iudeum ȝearpast cuðon;
þrunȝon þa on þreate þær on þrymme bád
330 in cynestole caseres mæȝ,
ȝeatolic ȝuðcpen ȝolde ȝehyrsted.
Elene maþelode 7 for eorlum spræc,
'Gehyrað hiȝeȝleaþe haliȝe rúne,
pord 7 pisdom; hpæt ȝe pitȝena
335 lare onfenȝon hu se líffruma
in cildes had cenned purde,
mihta pealdend be þam Moyses sanȝ
7 þæt [pord] ȝecpæð, peard Israhela,
"Eop acenned bið cniht on deȝle

(311) *on ȝedþeolan*] *7ȝedþeolan*. (318) *eopic*] *eop*. (338) *pord* not in MS.

(311) *Ȝedþeolan* could represent a case without a prep. or an adverbial use. But more probably the abbreviation 7 stands for *on*; cp *Gen.* 1879; *Cr. & Sat.* 502; Boethius, ed. Sedgefield 67, 24; *Pastoral Care* ed. Sweet (EETS 50) 486. Cp Kock, *Anglia* xliii, 302; Klaeber, *Anglia* xxix. 271.
(320a) Either a B half-line with stress on *þa* or for 'þa on ȝerum eodan' as Holthausen (*Elene* 1936) note to l. 320.
(339 ff) Isaiah vii, 14.

D

340 mihtum mære   spa þæs modor ne bið
    pæstmum ȝeeacnod   þurh peres friȝe."   fol. 124^b
    Be ðam Dauid cyninȝ   dryhtleoð áȝól,
    frod fyrnpeota,   fæder Salomones,
    7 þæt pord ȝecpæþ   piȝona baldor,

345 "Ic frumþa Ȝod   fore sceapode,
    siȝora dryhten;   he on ȝesyhðe pæs,
    mæȝena pealdend,   mín on þa spiðran,
    þrymmes hyrde;   þanon ic ne pen[d]o
    æfre to aldre   onsion mine."

350 Spa hit eft be eop   Essaias,
    pitȝa for peorodum   pordum mælde,
    deophycȝȝende   þurh dryhtnes ȝast,
    "Ic up ahóf   eaforan ȝinȝne
    7 bearn cende   þam ic blæd forȝeaf,

355 haliȝe hiȝefrofre;   ác hie hyrpdon [m]e
    feodon þurh feondscipe,   nahton foreþances,
    písdomes ȝepitt   7 þa pereȝan neat
    þe man daȝa ȝehpam   drifeð 7 þirsceð
    onȝitaþ hira ȝóddénd,   nales ȝnyrnpræcum

360 feoȝað frynd hiera   þe him fodder ȝifeð
    7 me Israhela   æfre ne poldon
    folc oncnapan   þeah ic feala for him
    æfter poruldstundum   pundra ȝefremede":7

.v.

HPÆT pe þæt ȝehyrdon   þurh haliȝe béc
365 þæt eop Dryhten ȝeaf   dóm unscyndne,
    meotod, mihta sped,   Moyse sæȝde
    hu ȝe heofoncyninȝe   hyran sceoldon,
    lare læstan.   Eop þæs lunȝre aþreat

(348) pendo] peno. (355) me] þe.

(345 ff) Ps. xv, 8.
(348b) Latin *commovear* suggests the emendation.
(353 ff) Isaiah i, 2–3. This text suggests Zupitza's emendation *eaforan ȝinȝe*.
(360) Ȝifeð: the singular is probably due to the indeclinable particle.

7 ʒe þam ryhte   piðroten hæfdon,
370 onscunedon þone sciran,   scippend, eallra dryhten,
7 ʒedpolan fylʒdon
ofer riht Godes.   Nu ʒe raþe ʒanʒaþ
7 findaþ ʒén   þa þe fyrnʒepritu
þurh snyttro cræft   selest cunnen,
375 æriht eoper   þæt me andspare
þurh sidne sefan   secʒan cunnen."
Eodan ða mid menʒo   mod[e] cpaniʒe,
collenferhðe   spa him sio cpen [be]béad;
fund[o]n þa fifhund   forþsnottera,
380 ales[o]n leodmæʒa   þa ðe leornunʒcræft
þurh modʒemynd   mæste hæfdon,
on sefan snyttro.   Heo to salore eft
ymb lytel fæc   laðode pæron,
ceastre peardas;   hio sio cpen onʒan
385 þordum ʒeneʒan—   plat ofer ealle—
'Oft ʒe dyslice   dæd ʒefremedon,
perʒe præcmæcʒʒas   7 ʒepritu herpdon,
fædera lare   næfre furður þonne nu   fol. 125[a]
ða ʒe blindnesse   bote forseʒon
390 7 ʒe piðsocon   soðe 7 rihte,
þæt in Bethleme   bearn pealdendes,
cyninʒ ánboren   cenned pære,
æðelinʒa ord;   þeah ʒe þa æ cuðon,

(377) *mode cpaniʒe*] *mod cpaniʒe*. (378) *bebead*] *bead*. (379) *fundon*]
funden. (380) *aleson*] *alesen*. (392) *pære*] *pære pære*.

(369b) *piðreotan* is a *hapax legomenon*. Since *piþ* is usually adversative
it presumably means 'be averse from', 'oppose'. This meaning is confirmed by the OHG gloss *aborretu uidharruzzit*; see Grein-Köhler, s.v.
wiðreotan.

(370) Most editors insert either *dryhtna* or *duʒuða* before *dryhten*
and read a full line with D alliteration in 371. But line 370 is made up
of parallel epithets like 1042. *Sciran* may be substantival, as *beorhtan*
in 782, or attributive. For scansion cp 891.

(377b) 'sad at heart'. Editors emend to *mode(s)cpan(i)ʒe*; Holthausen
(*Anglia* xxiii. 516) *modcpanʒe ʒuman*. The evidence of the rest of the
poem suggests that the spellings -*iʒe* for -*ʒe* are scribal, since they often
give a dissyllabic second sinking. Cp 57, 82, 121, 166, 314, 355, 478, 560,
762, 847, 977, 1214.

pitȝena pord   ȝe ne poldon þa,
395 synpyrcende   soð oncnapan.'
Hie þa ánmode   andsperedon,
'Hpæt pe Ebreisce   ǽ leornedon
þa on fyrndaȝum   fæderas cuðon
æt Ʒodes earce   ne pe eare cunnon
400 þurh hpæt ðu ðus hearde,   hlæfdiȝe, us
eorre purde;   þe ðæt æbylȝð nyton
þe þe ȝefremedon   on þysse folcscere,
þeodenbealpa   pið þec æfre'.
Elene maðelade   7 for eorlum spræc,
405 undearninȝa   ides reordode,
hlude for heriȝum,   'Ʒe nu hraðe ȝanȝað,
sundor ásecaþ   þa ðe snyttro mid eop,
mæȝn 7 modcræft   mæste hæbben
þæt me þinȝa ȝehpylc   þriste ȝecyðan,
410 untraȝlice   þe ic him to sece'.
Eodon þa fram rune   spa him sio rice cpen,
bald in burȝum   beboden hæfde,
ȝeomormode   ȝeorne smeadon,
sohton searoþancum   hpæt sio syn pære
415 þe hie on þam folce   ȝefremed hæfdon
pið þam casere   þe him sio cpen pite.
ȝa þær for eorlum   án reordode,
þidda ȝearosnotor   ðam pæs Iudas nama,
pordes cræftiȝ,   'Ic þat ȝeare
420 þæt hio pile secan   be ðam siȝebeame
on ðam þropode   þeoda paldend
eallra ȝnyrna leas,   Ʒodes aȝen bearn
þone [or]scyld[ne]   eofota ȝehpylces

(394) *e* of *pitȝena* above the line and a tag. (401) Maier reads *æby* (**ř** erasū) *lgð*. A point is used to connect the parts of the word separated by the erasure. (411) *cpen* on an erasure. (422) *ȝnyrna*] *ȝnyrnra*. (423) *orscyldne*] *scyldū*.

(401-3) æbylgð . . . þeodenbealpa: note the double construction after *pitan;* cp Kock, ESt xliv. 395; Kern, ESt li. 11.
(409) ȝecyðan: see note to line 82.
(423) For the emendation see Trautmann (BB xxiii. 99).

þurh hete henȝon   on heanne beam
425 in fyrndaȝum   fæderas usse.
    Þæt pæs þrealic ȝeþoht!   Nu is þearf mycel
    þæt we fæstlice ferhð staðelien
    þæt þe ðæs morðres   meldan ne peorðen
    hpær þæt haliȝe trio   beheled purde
430 æfter piȝþræce   þylæs toporpen sien
    frod fyrnȝepritu   ⁊ þa fæderlican
    lare forlet[e]n.   Ne bið lanȝ ofer ðæt
    þæt Israhela   æðelu moten
    ofer middanȝeard   má ricsian,
435 æcræft eorla   ȝif ðis yppe bið.
    Spa þa þæt ilce ȝio   mín yldra fæder
    siȝerof sæȝde—   þam pæs Sachius nama—
    frod fyrnpiota   fæder minum,
    [fæder min] eaferan;
440 pende hine of porulde   ⁊ þæt pord ȝecpæð,
    "Gif þe þæt ȝelimpe   on lifdaȝum
    þæt ðu ȝehyre   ymb þæt haliȝe treo
    frode friȝnan   ⁊ ȝeflitu ræran   fol. 125ᵇ
    be ðam siȝebeame   on þam soðcyninȝ
445 ahanȝen pæs,   heofonrices peard,
    eallre sybbe bearn   þonne þu snude ȝecyð,
    mín spæs sunu,   ær þec spylt nime.
    Ne mæȝ æfre ofer þæt   Ebrea þeod,
    rædþeahtende   rice healdan,
450 duȝuðum pealdan   ac þara dom leofað
    ⁊ hira dryhtscipe
    in poruld peorulda   pillum ȝefylled
    ðe þone ahanȝnan cyninȝ   heriaþ ⁊ lofiað":—

---

(424) A comma erased above and to the right of *þurh*. (432) *forleten*]
forleton. (439) *fæder min* not in MS. (453) *ðe* above the line and tag.

(432a) The MS reading may represent a nWS form of the past par-
ticiple; cp Sievers-Brunner § 366, 2 and line 971.

(438–9) The Latin has 'Avus meus praenuntiavit patri meo et pater
meus...adnuntiavit mihi dicens'... The emendation is based on the
assumption that the Old English had a similar expression which was
omitted by haplography. The construction is asyndetic. For the scansion
see PBB x. 483 and Das, *Cynewulf and the Cynewulf Canon* pp. 27, 125.

.vi.

Þa ic fromlice fæder minum,
455 ealdum æþitan áȝeaf andspare,
"Hu þolde þæt ȝepeorðan on þoruldrice
þæt on þone halȝan handa sendan
to feorhleȝe fæderas usse
þurh þrað ȝepitt ȝif hie þiston ǽr
460 þæt he Crist þære, cyninȝ on roderum,
soð sunu meotudes, sapla nerȝend?"
Ða me yldra mín aȝeaf andspare,
fród on fyrhðe fæder reordode,
"Onȝit ȝuma ȝinȝa Ȝodes heahmæȝen,
465 nerȝendes naman se is niða ȝehþam
unasecȝendlic þone sylf ne mæȝ
on moldpeȝe man aspyriȝean.
Næfre ic þa ȝeþeahte þe þeos þeod onȝan
secan þolde ac ic symle mec
470 ásced þara scylda, nales sceame þorhte
ȝaste minum; ic him ȝeorne oft
þæs unrihtes andsæc fremede
þonne uðþeotan æht bisæton,
on sefan sohton hu hie sunu meotudes
475 áhenȝon, helm þera, hlaford eallra
enȝla 7 elda, æðelust bearna.
Ne meahton hi[m] spa disiȝe deað oðfæstan
þeras þonsæliȝe spa hie þendon ær,
sarum settan, þeah he sume hpile
480 on ȝalȝan his ȝast onsende,
siȝebearn Godes; þa siððan þæs
of rode ahæfen rodera pealdend,
eallra þrymma þrym; þreo niht siððan
in byrȝenne bidende þæs
485 under þeosterlocan 7 þa þy þriddan dæȝ

(477) *him*] *hie.*

---

(459) þiston; see note to line 82.
(475) áhenȝon: see note to line 82.

44

ealles leohtes leoht   lifȝende áras,
ðeoden enȝla 7 his þeȝnum,
soð siȝora frea   seolfne ȝeypde,
beorht on blæde;   þonne broðor þin
490 onfenȝ æfter fyrste   fulpihtes bæð,
leohtne ȝeleafan;   þa for lufan dryhtnes
Stephanus þæs   stanum porpod;
ne ȝeald he yfel yfele   ac his ealdfeondum
þinȝode þrohtherd,   bæd þrymcyninȝ
495 þæt he him þa peadæd   to præce ne sette
þæt he for æfstum   unscyldiȝne,
synna leasne   Saples larum
feore beræddon;   spa he þurh feondscipe   fol. 126ᵃ
to cpale moniȝe   Cristes folces
500 demde to deaþe   spa þeah him dryhten eft
miltse ȝefremede   þæt he maneȝum [pearð]
folca to frofre;   syððan him frymða ȝod,
niða nerȝend   naman oncyrde
7 he syððan þæs   Sanctus Paulus
505 be naman haten   7 him næniȝ þæs
ǽlærendra   oðer betera
under speȝles hleo   syðþan æfre
þara þe pif oððe per   on poruld cendan
þeah he Stephanus   stanum hehte
510 ábreotan on beorȝe,   broðor þinne.
Nu ðu meaht ȝehyran,   hæleð mín se leofa,
hu árfæst is   ealles pealdend
þeah pe æbylȝð pið hine   oft ȝepyrcen,
synna punde   ȝif þe sona eft
515 þara bealudæda   bote ȝefremmaþ
7 þæs unrihtes   eft ȝespicaþ.
Forðan ic soðlice   7 mín spæs fæder

(501) *pearð* not in MS.

(487b) The MS reading gives a very weak half-line with vowel alliteration. Dr Brooks has suggested to me that the correct reading is '7 þeȝnum his' which seems probable.

(508) Note the lack of concord. For the congruence of compound subjects see Bauch, *op.cit.* 63.

syðþan ʒelyfdon
þæt ʒeþropade   eallra þrymma ʒod,
520 lifes láttiop   laðlic píte
for oferþearfe   ilda cynnes.

Forðan ic þe lære   þurh leoðorune,
hyse leofesta,   þæt ðu hospcpide,
æfst ne eofulsæc   æfre ne fremme,
525 ʒrimne ʒeaʒncpide   pið ʒodes bearne;
þonne ðu ʒeearnast   þæt þe bið ece líf,
selust siʒeleana   seald in heofonum.'
Ðus mec fæder mín   on fyrndaʒum
unpeaxenne   pordum lærde,
530 septe soðcpidum—   þam þæs Symon nama—
ʒuma ʒehdum fród.   Nu ʒe ʒeare cunnon
hpæt eop þæs on sefan   selest þince
to ʒecyðanne   ʒif ðeos cpen usic
friʒneð ymb ðæt treo   nu ʒe fyrhðsefan
535 7 modʒeþanc   minne cunnon'.

Him þa toʒenes   þa ʒleapestan
on pera þreate   pordum mældon,
'Næfre we hyrdon   hæleð æniʒne
on þysse þeode   butan þec nuða,
540 þeʒn oðerne   þyslic cyðan
ymb spa dyʒle pyrd;   do spa þe þynce,

(524) Maier thought that two letters, perhaps *ne*, had been erased
after *fremme*. (526) Two letters, read by Maier as *ya?*, erased before
ece. (531) An erasure after *fród*.

---

(521) oferþearfe: 'great need'. The use of *ofer-* in this sense may be
due to Latin influence. See Baxter and Johnson, *Medieval Latin Word-
List* s.v. *super-*.

(522) leoðorune: cp 1250 *leoðucræft*; the emended forms *leoðrune*,
leoðcræft are probably to be preferred although the form *leoðocræft*
may be compared with *leoðufæst* 'skilful'. Cp *Beo.* 2769, *leoðocræftum*
'skilfully'.

(531) gehdum: Zupitza emended to *giddum* but the phrase may mean
'well-versed in sorrow', 'wise'; cp *Beo.* 3095 and Klaeber, ESt lv. 284;
Kern, *Taalkundige Bijdragen* i. 208–9.

(534a) For the scansion see Klaeber, *Beowulf* (1941) p. 279. But the
line is readily emended to *ymb ðæt treo friʒneð*.

fyrnȝidda frod,   ȝif ðu fruȝnen sie
on þera corðre.   Þisdomes beðearf,
þorda þærlicra   7 þitan snyttro
545 se ðære æðelan sceal   andþyrde aȝifan
for þyslicne   þreat on meþle':—

.vii.

ÞEOXan þordcþidum,   þeras þeahtedon
on healfa ȝehþær   sume hyder sume þyder,
þrydedon 7 þohton;   þa cþom þeȝna heap
550 to þam heremeðle,   hreopon friccan,
caseres bodan,   'Eoþ þeos cþen laþaþ,   fol. 126ᵇ
secȝas to salore   þæt ȝe seonoðdomas
rihte reccen;   is eoþ rædes þearf,
on meðelstede   modes snyttro'.

555 Heo þæron ȝearþe,   ȝeomormode
leodȝebyrȝean   þa hie laðod þæron
þurh heard ȝebann;   to hofe eodon,
cyðdon cræftes miht.   Þa sio cþen onȝan
þeras Ebresce   þordum neȝan,
560 fricȝȝan fyrhðþeriȝe   ymb fyrnȝeþritu
hu on þorulde ær   pitȝa[n] sunȝon,
ȝasthaliȝe ȝuman   be Jodes bearne
hþær se þeoden   ȝeþroþade,
soð sunu meotudes   for saþla lufan.

565 Heo þæron stearce,   stane heardran,
noldon þæt ȝeryne   rihte cyðan
ne hire andspare   æniȝe secȝan,
tornȝeniðlan   þæs hio him to sohte

(561) *pitȝan*] *pitȝa.*

(547a) Cosijn, *Tijdschrift voor Nederlandsche Taal- en Letterkunde* i
144 reads *prixledan* supposing confusion arose from an original northern
peoxledan; cp *prixlan ȝiddum*; *þordum prixlan.* But the idiom here is not
impossible. Grimm compares *Heliand* 5969 f. 'bigunnun im quidi managa
wahsan'. The subject however is 'they' not 'words', since the metre
requires *þordcþidum* as a compound. *Arngart* (*op.cit.* 20) compares
M.N.D. II i. 56 '(they) waxen in their mirth'.

ac hio porda ӡehpæs   piðersæc fremedon,
570 fæste on fyrhðe   þæt heo friӡnan onӡan,
cpædon þæt hio on aldre   opiht spylces
ne ær ne sið   æfre hyrdon.
Elene maþelade   7 him yrre oncpæð,
'Ic eop to soðe   secӡan pille
575 7 þæs in life   liӡe ne pyrðeð
ӡif ӡe þissum lease   lenӡ ӡefylӡað,
mid fæcne ӡefice,   þe me fore standaþ
þæt eop in beorӡe   bǽl fornimeð,
hattost heaðopelma   7 eoper hra bryttað,
580 lacende liӡ   þæt eop sceal þæt leas ápundrad
peorðan to poruldӡedale.   Ne maӡon ӡe ða pord
   ӡeseðan
þe ӡe hpile nú on unriht
priӡon under pomma sceatum;   ne maӡon ӡe þa pyrd
   bemiðan,
bedyrnan þa deopan mihte'.   Ða purdon hie deaðes
   on penan,
585 ádes 7 endelifes–   7 þær þa ænne betæhton
ӡiddum ӡearusnottorne—   þam pæs Iudas nama
cenned for cneomaӡum—   þone hie þære cpene aӡefon,
sæӡdon hine sundorpisne,   'He þe mæӡ soð ӡecyðan,
onpreon pyrda ӡeryno   spa ðu hine pordum friӡnest,
590 ǽriht from ord[e]   oð ende forð;

(590) *orde*] *ord*.

(578b) Frucht's reading 'bælfyr nimeð' is unnecessary (*Metrisches u. Sprachliches zu Cy's El.* 30). Cp Ælfric *Hom.* ed. Thorpe i. 322: 'God is spa spa Paulus cpæð, fornymende fyr' from Heb. xii, 29 'Etenim deus noster ignis consumens est'. For the scansion see PBB x. 230–2.

(580) Thorpe's false reading *apundrad* for the MS. *apundrad*, was adopted as an emendation by Grein-Wülcker; Grimm suggested *apended*; Strunk, MLN xvii. 373, *asundrad*. But *apundrad* may mean 'considered'. *Pundernian* and *apyndrian* seem to mean 'weigh', but the metaphorical sense appears in *pundere* 'scholar'; OF *ponderer*, whence ModE 'ponder', may have merely reinforced an existing sense of an OE *apundrian*. Translate 'that lie shall be accounted to you worthy of death'? Most editors end line 580 after *leas* but a half-line makes this unnecessary.

(590) orde oð ende: cp Onions, MLR xxiv. 389–93.

he is for eorðan æðeles cynnes,
þordcræftes þis 7 pitȝan sunu,
bald on meðle; him ȝebyrde is
þæt he ȝencpidas ȝleape hæbbe,
595 cræft in breostum; he ȝecyðeð þe
for þera menȝo þisdomes ȝife
þurh þa myclan miht spa þín mod lufaþ'.
Hio on sybbe forlet secan ȝehpylcne
aȝenne eard 7 þone ænne ȝenam
600 Iudas to ȝisle 7 þa ȝeorne bæd   fol. 127ᵃ
þæt he be ðære rode riht ȝetæhte
þe ær in leȝere þæs lanȝe bedyrned
7 hine seolfne sundor aciȝde.
Elene maþelode to þam ánhaȝan,
605 tíreadiȝ cpen, 'þe synt tu ȝearu,
spa líf spa deað spa þe leofre bið
to ȝeceosanne; cyð ricene nu
hpæt ðu þæs to þinȝe þafian pille'.
Iudas hire onȝen þinȝode— ne meahte he þa ȝehðu
    bebuȝan,
610 oncyrran [cyninȝ] ȝeniðlan, he þæs on þære cpene
    ȝepealdum—
'Hu mæȝ þæm ȝepeorðan þe on þestenne
meðe 7 meteleas mórland trydeð,
hunȝre ȝehæfted 7 him hlaf 7 stan
on ȝesihðe bú ȝepeorðað
615 stea[r]c 7 hnesce, þæt he þone stan nime
þið hunȝres hleo, hlafes ne ȝime,

(599) an erasure after the first *n* of *aȝenne*.
(610) *cyninȝ*] *rex*. (615) *stearc*] *streac*.

---

(608) *þæs to þinȝe*: 'as a condition', viz. 'which alternative will you choose?'

(610) For the reading *cyninȝ* see Holthausen, Anglia Beibl xxi. 174. Cp 1041.

(614) Most editors add a word before *ȝepeorðað*; Zupitza suggests *samod ȝepeorðað*; Klaeber, JEGP xviii. 252 *ȝeseted þeorðað*.

(615) For the form *streac* compare *Andreas* 196 *sæstearmas*; and, perhaps, *Andreas* 1313 *ȝescyrded*.

ʒepende to pædle   7 þa þiste piðsæce,
beteran piðhyccʒe   þonne he beʒa beneah':—

.viii.

HIM þa seo eadiʒe   andpyrde áʒeaf,
620 Elene for eorlum   undearnunʒa,
    'Gif ðu in heofonrice   habban pille
    eard mid enʒlum   7 on eorðan líf,
    siʒorlean in speʒle,   saʒa ricene me
    hpær seo rod puniʒe   radorcyninʒes,
625 haliʒ under hrusan   þe ʒe hpile nú
    þurh morðres mán   mannum dyrndun.
    Iudas maðelade—   him þæs ʒeomor sefa,
    hat æt heortan   7 ʒehpæðres pá
    ʒe h[im] heofonrices   [hador] spamode,
630 7 þis andpearde   ánforlete,
    rice under roderum,   ʒ[if] he ða rode ne tæhte—
    'Hu mæʒ ic þæt findan   þæt spa fyrn ʒepearð
    pintra ʒanʒum?   Is nu porn sceacen
    tu hund oððe ma   ʒeteled rime;
635 ic ne mæʒ areccan   nu ic þæt rim ne can;

(629a) *him*] *he*. (629b) *hador* not in MS. (631) *ʒif*] *ʒe*.

(628–31) The Latin has 'Si ergo in caelo et in terra vis vivere, dic mihi, ubi absconditum est lignum pretiosae crucis'. The sense of the English is thus that, if Judas conceals the whereabouts of the cross, his affliction will be twofold: his body will die and his soul will perish in hell. *Ʒe* in 631 is thus inappropriate and Trautmann's reading *ʒif* in BB xxiii. 103 has been adopted. MS *spamode* could represent a verb *spæman* by confusion of *spa* and *spæ*, for, although the simplex does not occur in OE, ME *spemen* suggests a transitive verb 'grieve'. It would then be possible to keep MS *he* and read 'ʒe he heofonrices hlaford spæmde'. But the reading in the text, an adaptation of Zupitza's 'hyht spamode', has in its favour the retention of the MS reading. Translate 'his was a sorrowful heart. . .a double woe: the light of heaven would grow dim for him and he would leave this present (light), the world under the heavens, if he did not reveal the cross'. The subject of *anforlete* is to be understood from *him*; cp Pogatscher, *Anglia* xxiii. 280. For *hador* as a noun see Klaeber, *Beowulf* (1941) 142.

is nu feal[a] siðþan   forð ȝepitenra,
frodra 7 ȝodra   þe us fore pæron
ȝleapra ȝumena;   ic on ȝeoȝoðe pearð
on siðdaȝum   syððan acenned
640 cnihtȝeonȝ hæleð;   ic ne can þæt ic nat
findan on fyrhðe   þæt spa fyrn ȝepearð'.
Elene maðelade   him on andspare,
'Hu is þæt ȝeporden   on þysse perþeode
þæt ȝe spa moniȝfeald   on ȝemynd piton
645 alra tacna ȝehpylc spa Troian[æ]
þurh ȝefeoht fremedon?   Þæt pæs f[ie]r myc[le],
open ealdȝepin   þonne þeos æðele ȝepyrd,
ȝeara ȝonȝum;   ȝe þæt ȝeare cunnon
edre ȝereccan   hpæt þær eallra pæs
650 on manrime   morðorslehtes,   fol. 127ᵇ
dareðlacendra   deadra ȝefeallen
under bordhaȝan;   ȝe þa byrȝenna
under stanhleoðum   7 þa stope spa some
7 þa pinterȝerím   on ȝepritu setton'.
655 Iudas maðelade—   ȝnornsorȝe pæȝ—
'Þe þæs herepeorces,   hlæfdiȝe mín,
for nydþearfe   nean myndȝiaþ
7 þa piȝȝþræce   on ȝepritu setton,
þeoda ȝebæru   7 þis næfre
660 þurh æniȝes mannes   muð ȝehyrdon,
hæleðu[m] cyðan   butan her nuða.
Him seo æðele cpen   aȝeaf andspare,

(636) *feala*] *feale*. (637) An erasure between *us* and *fore*. (640) Second
ic above the line and a tag. (645) *Troianæ*] *troiana*. (646) *fier mycle*] *fær
mycel*. (661) *hæleðum*] *hæleðu*. (662) Maier read *7spáre*.

(645a) tacna: here 'wonder', 'heroic deed'. Cp Grk. σημεῖον 'sign',
'work of power'.

(645b) For the plural of tribal names in -*æ*, Lat. -*i* see Orosius, ed.
Sweet (EETS 79) 78, 6; 56, 14.

(646b) *mycel* for *mycle* in a comparative construction has been thought
possible; cp *Beo.* 69–70. Such a construction might explain the substitution of *fær* for the necessary comparative. *þonne* can hardly mean 'then'
as suggested by Imelmann in Anglia Beibl xvii. 226; cp, also, Koeppel,
ESt xxx. 376–7. Translate 'that was much longer ago'.

'Þiðsæcest ðu to spiðe soðe 7 rihte
ymb þæt lifes treop 7 nu lytle ær
665 sæȝdest soðlice be þam siȝebeame
leodum þinum 7 nu on liȝe cyrrest'.
Iudas hire onȝen þinȝode, cpæð þæt he þæt on ȝehðu
ȝespræce
7 tpeon spiðost, þende him traȝe hnaȝre.
Him oncpæð hraðe caseres mæȝ,
670 'Hpæt þe ðæt hyrdon þurh haliȝe bec
hæleðum cyðan þæt ahanȝen pæs
on Caluarie cyninȝes freobearn,
Ȝodes ȝastsunu; þu scealt ȝeaȝninȝa
pisdom onpreon spa ȝepritu secȝaþ
675 æfter stedepanȝe, hpær seo stop sie,
Caluar[i]e ær þec cpealm nime,
spilt for synnum þæt ic hie syððan mæȝe
ȝeclænsian Criste to þillan,
hæleðum to helpe þæt me haliȝ Ȝod
680 ȝefylle, frea mihtiȝ, feores inȝeþanc,
peoruda puldorȝeofa, þillan minne,
ȝasta ȝeocend'. Hire Iudas oncpæð
stiðhycȝende, 'Ic þa stope ne can
ne þæs panȝes piht ne þa pisan cann'.
685 Elene maðelode þurh eorne hyȝe,
'Ic þæt ȝesperiȝe þurh sunu meotodes,
þone áhanȝan ȝod þæt ðu hunȝre scealt
for cneomaȝum cpylmed peorðan
butan þu forlæte þa leasunȝa
690 7 me speotollice soð ȝecyðe'.
Heht þa spa cpicne corðre lædan,
scufan scyldiȝne— scealcas ne ȝældon—
in drýȝne seað þær he duȝuða leas
siomode in sorȝum seofon nihta fyrst

(671) the first *n* of *ahanȝen* above the line and a tag. (676) *Caluarie*]
caluare.

(668a) Understand the preposition from 'on ȝehðu' or expand 7 to
on as in 311.

695 under hearmlocan   hunʒre ʒeþreatod,
clommum beclunʒen   7 þa cleopiʒan onʒan
sarum besylced   on þone seofeðan dæʒ,
meðe 7 meteleas—   mæʒen þæs ʒespiðrod—
'Ic eop healsie   þurh heofona Ʒod
700 þæt ʒe me of ðyssum earfeðum   up forlæten,
heanne fram hunʒres ʒeniðlan;   ic þæt haliʒe treo
lustum cyðe   nu ic hit lenʒ ne mæʒ
helan for hunʒre;   is þes hæft to ðan stranʒ, fol. 128ᵃ
þreanyd þæs þearl   7 þes þroht to ðæs heard
705 doʒorrimum;   ic adreoʒan ne mæʒ
ne lenʒ helan   be ðam lifes treo
þeah ic ær mid dysiʒe   þurhdrifen pære
7 ðæt soð to late   seolf ʒecneope':—. viiii.

ÞA ðæt ʒehyrde   sio þær hæleðum scead,
710 beornes ʒebæro   hio bebead hraðe
þæt hine man of nearpe   7 of nydcleofan,
fram þam énʒan hofe   up forlete.
Hie ðæt ofstlice   efnedon sona
7 hine mid arum   up ʒelæddon
715 of carcerne   spa him seo cpén bebead.
Stopon þa to þære stope   stiðhycʒende
on þa dune úp   ðe dryhten ǽr
ahanʒen þæs   heofonrices peard,
ʒodbearn on ʒálʒan   7 hpæðre ʒeare nyste,
720 hunʒre ʒehyned   hpær sio haliʒ[e] ród
þurh [facen]searu   foldan ʒetyned,
lanʒe leʒere fæst,   leodum dyrne,
punode pælreste.   Þord stunde ahof
elnes oncyðiʒ   7 on Ebrisc spræc,

(715) *bebead* with the prefix above the line and a tag. (716) *stope stið* on an erasure. (718) Erasure after *pæs*. (720) *haliʒe*] *haliʒ*. (721) *facensearu*] *searu*.

(717) ðe: 'on which'; cp Kern, ESt li. 12 and lines 162, 416.
(721a) For the emendation see Paris-Psalter lv. 1.
(724a) BT equate with *uncyðiʒ* 'weak', 'ignorant' but the presumable connection with German *Ankündigung*, OE *ncyðan*, makes this unlikely. Translate 'revealing courage', 'bold'. Cp 960.

725 'Dryhten Hælend, þu ðe ahst doma ӡepeald
7 þu ӡeporhtest   þurh þines puldres miht
heofon 7 eorðan   7 holmþræce,
sæs sidne fæðm   samod ealle ӡesceaft,
7 þu amæte   mundum þinum

730 ealne ymbhpyrft   7 úprador
7 þu sylf sitest,   siӡora paldend
ofer þam æðelestan   enӡelcynne
þe ӡeond lyft farað   leohte bepundene,
mycle mæӡenþrymme;   ne mæӡ þær manna ӡecynd

735 of eorðpeӡum   úp ӡeferan
in lichoman   mid þa leohtan ӡedryht,
puldres aras;   þu ӡeporhtest þa
7 to þeӡnunӡe   þinre ӡesettest,
haliӡ 7 heofonlic;   þara on hade sint

740 in sindreame   syx ӡenemned
þa ymbsealde synt   mid syxum eac
fiðrum, ӡefrætpad;   fæӡere scínaþ;
þara si[n]t feoper   þe on flihte á
þa þeӡnunӡe   þrymme bepeotiӡaþ

745 fore onsyne   eces deman,
sinӡallice   sinӡaþ in puldre
hædrum stefnum   heofoncininӡes lof,
poða pliteӡaste   7 þas pord cpeðaþ
clænum stefnum—   þam is Ceruphin nama—

750 "Haliӡ is se halӡa   heahenӡla Ӡod,
peoroda pealdend;   is ðæs puldres ful
heofun 7 eorðe   7 eall heahmæӡen
tire ӡetacnod";   syndon tú on þam,
siӡorcynn on speӡle   þe man Seraphin

755 be naman hateð;   he sceal Neorxnapanӡ

---

(731) An erasure (according to Maier *on*) before *siӡora*. The *o* of *siӡora* above the line. (734) *mæӡen þrymme* above the line probably in a later hand. But cp Sisam, *Studies* 113. (743) *sint*] *sit*.

(739) þara on hade: 'in which order'.
(755) Some editors emend 'he sceal' to 'hie sculon' but one angel only may be intended as Grein-Wülcker (169) suggest. Or *he* is written for *hie* whence the singular verb.

7 lifes treo leȝene speorde
haliȝ healdan. Heardecȝ cpacaþ,
beofaþ broȝdenmǽl 7 bleom prixleð
ȝrapum ȝryrefæst; þæs ðu, ȝod dryhten,
760 pealdest pidan fyrhð 7 þu pomfulle,
scyldpyrcende, sceaðan of radorum
apurpe, ponhydiȝe; þa sio perȝe sceolu
under heolstorhofu hreosan sceolde
in pita forpyrd þær hie in pylme nu
765 dreoȝaþ deaðcpale in dracan fæðme
þeostrum forþylmed. He þinum piðsóc
aldordome; þæs he in ermðum sceal
ealra fula ful fáh þropian,
þeopned þolian. Þær he þín ne mæȝ
770 pord ápeorpan, is in pitum fæst
ealre synne fruma susle ȝebunden.
Ȝif þin pilla sie, pealdend enȝla,
þæt ricsie se ðe on rode pæs
7 þurh Marian in middanȝeard
775 acenned pearð in cildes had,
þeoden enȝla— ȝif he þin nære,
sunu synna leas næfre he soðra spa feala,
in poruldrice, pundra ȝefremede
doȝorȝerimum no ðu of deaðe hine
780 spa þrymlice, þeoda pealdend,
apeahte for peorodum ȝif he in puldre þin
þurh ða beorhtan bearn ne pære—
ȝedo nu, fæder enȝla, forð beacen þín;
spa ðu ȝehyrdest þone halȝan per,

(757) *ecȝ* above the line and tag. (767) *he* may have an accent but the mark seems to have been incised and has not the usual thickness at the top. (771) The *s* of *susle* has been squeezed between the *u* and the *l*.

(763a) Most editors read *heolstorhofu* but the metre suggests that *heolstor* may be an adjective. Cp, however, PBB x. 481.

(765) dracan fæðme: see Jonah ii, 2.

(768) ealra fula ful: an extension of such phrases as 'eallra þrymma þrym'. These are probably an imitation of the biblical use of an intensive genitive. Cp 733.

785 Moyses on meðle þa ðu, mihta ʒod,
ʒehypdest þam eorle on þa æðelan tíd
under beorhhliðe bán Iosephes
spa ic þe, þeroda Þyn, ʒif hit sie þilla þín,
þurʒ þæt beorhte ʒesceap biddan þille

790 þæt me þæt ʒoldhord ʒasta scyppend
ʒeopenie þæt yldum þæs
lanʒe behyded. Forlæt nú, lifes Fruma,
of ðam þanʒstede þynsumne úp,
under radores ryne, rec astiʒan

795 lyftlacende; ic ʒelyfe þe sel
7 þy fæstlicor ferhð staðeliʒe,
hyht untþeondne on þone ahanʒnan Crist
þæt he sie soðlice saþla nerʒend,
éce ælmihtiʒ, Israhela cininʒ,

800 þalde þidan ferhð þuldres on heofenum
á butan ende ecra ʒestealda':—

.x.

ÐA of ðære stoþe steam úp aras
spylce réc under radorum. Þær aræred pearð
beornes breostsefa; he mid bæm handum

805 eadiʒ 7 æʒleap uppeard þleʒade.
Iudas maþelode ʒleap in ʒeþance,
'Nu ic þurh soð hafu seolf ʒecnaþen
on heardum hiʒe þæt ðu hælend eart   fol. 129ᵃ
middanʒeardes; sie ðe mæʒena ʒod

810 þrymsittendum þanc butan ende
þæs ðu me spa meðum 7 spa mánþeorcum

(810) An *m* has been erased after *þrym*.

---

(787) A reference to a Talmudic legend according to which Joseph's
bones, concealed either in the Nile or among the royal tombs, are
miraculously revealed by Moses' prayers. See Emerson, MLN xiv.
331–4.
(805) Judas clapped his hands; cp Junius Psalter xlvi. 1, *plaudite
manibus* 'pleʒiað ʒe mid hondum'. The Latin has *et plauderet ambis
manibus*.

þurh þin puldor inpriȝe   pyrda ȝeryno.
Nu ic þe, bearn Ȝodes,   biddan pille,
peoroda pillȝifa,   nu ic pat þæt ðu eart
815 ȝecyðed 7 acenned   allra cyninȝa þrym
þæt ðu ma ne sie   minra ȝylta
þara þe ic ȝefremede   nalles feam siðum,
metud, ȝemyndiȝ.   Læt mec, mihta Ȝod,
on rimtale   rices þines
820 mid haliȝra   hlyte puniȝan
in þære beorhtan byriȝ,   þær is broðor mín
ȝepeorðod in puldre   þæs he þære pið þec,
Stephanus, heold   þeah he stanȝreopum
porpod þære.   He hafað piȝȝes lean,
825 blæd butan blinne;   sint in bocum his
pundor þa he porhte   on ȝepritum cyðed.
Onȝan þa pilfæȝen   æfter þam puldres treo
elnes ánhydíȝ   eorðan delfan
under turfhaȝan   þæt he on tpentiȝum
830 fotmælum feor   funde behelede,
under neolum niðer   næsse ȝehydde,
in þeostorcofan—   he ðær þreo mette—
in þam reonian hofe,   roda ætsomne,
ȝreote beȝrauene,   spa hio ȝeardaȝum
835 arleasra sceolu   eorðan beþeahton,
Iudea [cyn];   hie pið Ȝodes bearne
nið áhofun   spa hie no sceoldon
þær hie leahtra fruman   larum ne hyrdon.
Þa pæs modȝemynd   myclum ȝeblissod,
840 hiȝe onhyrded   þurh þæt haliȝe treo,

(836) *cyn* not in MS.

(812b) 'disclose the hidden things of God's Providence'. Cp Timmer,
Neophilologus xxvi. 24–33; 213–28.

(826b) viz. in Acts.

(827–36) Krapp (*Vercelli Book*) suggests a stop after *þeostorcofan*,
and presumably takes *þæt* as relative with antecedent *treo*. But the
syntax of *behelede* and *ȝehydde* is then difficult. Holthausen (*Elene* 1936)
implies that 827–36 is an anacoluthon, since he puts a dash after
þeostorcofan. But parenthesis in 832b gives a clearer construction.

inbryrded breostsefa   syððan beacen ʒeseh
haliʒ under hrusan;   he mid handum befenʒ
puldres pynbeam   7 mid peorode áhóf
of foldʒræfe.   Feðeʒestas
845   eodon, æðelinʒas   in on þa ceastre.
Ásetton þa on ʒesyhðe   siʒebeamas þrie
eorlas anhydiʒe   fore Elenan cneo,
collenferhðe;   cpen peorces ʒefeah
on ferhðsefan   7 þa friʒnan onʒan
850   on hpylcum þara beama   bearn pealdendes,
hæleða hyhtʒifa   hanʒen pære,
'Hpæt þe þæt hyrdon   þurh haliʒe bec
tacnum cyðan   þæt tpeʒen mid him
ʒeþropedon   7 he þæs þridda sylf
855   on rode treo;   rodor eal ʒespearc
on þa sliðan tíd;   saʒa ʒif ðu cunne
on hpylcre þyssa þreora   þeoden enʒla,
ʒeþropode,   þrymmes hyrde'.   fol. 129^b
Ne meahte hire Iudas—   ne ful ʒere piste—
860   speotole ʒecyþan   be ðam siʒebeame,
on hpylcre se hælend   áhafen pære,
siʒebearn ʒodes   ær he asettan heht
on þone middel   þære mæran byriʒ
beamas mid bearhtme   7 ʒebidan þær
865   oððæt him ʒecyðde   cyninʒ ælmihtiʒ
pundor for peorodum   be ðam puldres treo.
ʒesæton siʒerofe,   sanʒ áhofon
ræd þeahtende   ymb þa roda þreo
oð þa niʒoðan tíd;   hæfdon neopne ʒefean
870   mærðum ʒemeted;   þa þær meniʒo cpom,
folc unlytel 7   ʒefærenne man
brohton on bære   beorna þreate

(841–2) *seh* above the line and a tag; comma erased after *beacen*;
both *beacen* and first letter of *ʒeseh* on an erasure. (847) The *n* of *cneo*
above the line and a tag.

(855) Three or four letters erased after *rode*.

(861) *hpylcre* may be a mistake for *hpylcne* or due to the poet's
having thought of *rod* rather than *siʒebeam* as the antecedent.

on neapeste— pæs þa niᵹoðe tid—
ᵹinᵹne ᵹastleasne. Þa ðær Iudas pæs
875 on modsefan miclum ᵹeblissod.
Heht þa asettan saplleasne,
life belidenes lic, on eorðan,
unlifᵹendes, ⁊ up áhof
rihtes pemend þara roda tpa,
880 fyrhðᵹleap on fæðme ofer þæt fæᵹe hús,
deophycᵹende; hit pæs dead spa ær,
lic leᵹere fæst, leomu colodon
þreanedum beþeaht; þa sio þridde pæs
áhafen haliᵹ; hrá pæs on anbide
885 oððæt him uppan æðelinᵹes pæs
ród áræred, rodorcyninᵹes beam,
siᵹebeacen soð; he sona aras
ᵹaste ᵹeᵹearpod, ᵹeador bú samod
lic ⁊ sapl. Þær pæs lof hafen
890 fæᵹer mid þy folce, fæder peorðodon
⁊ þone soðan, sunu pealdendes
pordum heredon. Sie him puldor ⁊ þanc
a butan ende eallra
        ᵹesceafta:—
ÐA pæs þam folce on ferhðsefan
895 inᵹemynde— spa him a scyle—
pundor þa þe porhte peoroda dryhten
to feorhnere fira cynne,
lifes lattiop. Þa þær liᵹesynniᵹ
on lyft astah lacende feond.
900 Onᵹan þa hleoðrian helle deofol,
eatol æclæca yfela ᵹemyndiᵹ,
'Hpæt is þis, la, manna þe minne eft
þurh fyrnᵹeflit folᵹaþ pyrdeð,

---

(873) Maier read *tíd*. (877) An erasure of four or five letters between
belidenes and *lic*. (878) An erasure between the *n* and *l* of *unlifᵹendes*.
(898) *lattiop*'.

(884b) The body was in suspense waiting for the return of the soul.
For the scansion see Das, *op.cit*. 21, 239.

íceð ealdne nið, æhta strudeð?

905 Þis is sinʒal sacu; sapla ne moton,
mánfremmende in minum lenʒ
æhtum puniʒan; nu cpom elþeodiʒ
þone ic ær on firenum fæstne talde,
hafað mec bereafod ríhta ʒehpylces,

910 feohʒestreona; nis ðæt fæʒer sið.
Feala me se hælend hearma ʒefremede,
niða nearolicra, se ðe in Nazareð
afeded pæs; syððan furþum peox   fol. 130ᵃ
of cildhade symle cirde to him

915 æhte mine; ne mot æniʒe nu
rihte spopan; is his rice brad
ofer middanʒeard, min is ʒespiðrod,
ræd under roderum; ic þa rode ne þearf
hleahtre heriʒean; hpæt, se hælend me

920 in þam enʒan ham oft ʒetynde
ʒeomrum to sorʒe. Ic þurh Iudas ær
hyhtful ʒepearð 7 nu ʒehyned eom
ʒóda ʒeasne þurh Iudas eft,
fáh 7 freondleas; ʒen ic findan can

925 þúrh prohtstafas piðercyr pið ðan
of ðam pearhtreafum; ic apecce pið ðe
oðerne cyninʒ se ehteð þin
7 he forlæteð lare þine
7 manþeapum minum folʒaþ

930 ond þec þonne sendeð in þa speartestan
7 þa pyrrestan pitebroʒan
þæt ðu sarum forsoht piðsæcest fæste
þone ahanʒnan cyninʒ þam ðu hyrdest ær'.
Him ða ʒleaphydiʒ Iudas oncpæð,

935 hæleð hildedeor— him pæs Haliʒ Ȝast
befolen fæste, fyrhat lufu,

---

(924) can] ne can. (926). apecce] ǽpecce.

(925b) pið ðan: 'against that'; see Sisam, RES xxii. 267.
(927a) Julian the Apostate under whom Judas is said to have suffered martyrdom.

peallende ȝepitt, þurh Þiȝan snyttro—
7 þæt pord ȝecpæð pisdomes ful,
'Ne þearft ðu spa spiðe synna ȝemyndiȝ

940 sár nipiȝan 7 sæce ræran,
morðres mánfrea; þ[ec] se mihtiȝa cyninȝ
in neolnesse nyðer bescufeð
synpyrcende, in susla ȝrund,
domes leasne, se ðe deadra feala

945 porde apehte; pite ðu þe ȝearpor
þæt ðu unsnyttrum ánforlete
leohta beorhtost 7 lufan dryhtnes,
þone fæȝran ȝefean 7 on fyrbæðe
suslum beþrunȝen syððan punodest,

950 ade onæled 7 þær apa scealt,
piðerhycȝende, perȝðu dreoȝan,
yrmðu butan ende'. Elene ȝehyrde
hu se feond 7 se freond ȝeflitu rærdon,
tíreadiȝ 7 traȝ on tpa halfa,

955 synniȝ 7 ȝesæliȝ; sefa pæs þe ȝlædra
þæs þe heo ȝehyrde þone helle sceaþan
oferspiðende, synna bryttan
7 þa pundrade ymb þæs peres snyttro,
hu he spa ȝeleafful, on spa lytlum fæce—

960 7 spa uncyðiȝ— æfre purde,

941 þec] þæt. (952) An erasure between *butan* and *ende*. (954) The *l*
of *halfa* above the line. (958) The *b* of *ymb* above the line and a tag.

(937b) The Latin has 'Iudas autem fervens in SS., dixit'... The
traditional emendation *pitȝa* is thus unsuitable. It is tempting to
speculate that *piȝa* might here be a weak noun from OE *pih* and thus
'The Holy One'. The existence of the more common homonym *piȝa*
'warrior' would explain its disuse. Cp Williams, *The Conflict of Homonyms
in English*.

(941b) See Cosijn, *Aanteekeningen op den Beowulf* 32.

(957a) Most editors read *oferswiðedne* (cp VPs 125, 1?). The emendation should probably be accepted.

(960) *uncyðiȝ* is usually emended to *oncyðiȝ* (cp *unforht* in *Dream of
the Rood* 117). If the prefix is privative or pejorative, the translation may
be 'how he became, in so short a time, and ignorant *or* wicked as he was,
so full of faith'. For the construction cp 'spa disiȝe' 477; 'spa cþicne' 691
and NED *so* 14.

ȝleapnesse þurhȝoten;   Ᵹode þancode,
puldorcyninȝe   þæs hire se pilla ȝelamp
þurh bearn Ᵹodes   beȝa ȝehpæðres,
ȝe æt þære ȝesyhðe   þæs siȝebeames,
965   ȝe ðæs ȝeleafan   þe hio spa leohte oncneop,
puldorfæste ȝife   in þæs peres breostum:—

ÐA þæs ȝefreȝe   in þære folcsceare,   fol. 130ᵇ
ȝeond þa perþeode   pide læded
mære morȝenspel   maniȝum on andan
970   þara þe dryhtnes ǽ   dyrnan poldon,
bod[e]n æfter burȝum   spa brimo fæðm[a]ð
in ceastra ȝehpære   þæt Cristes [rod]
fyrn foldan beȝræfen   funden pære,
selest siȝebeacna   þara þe sið oððe ær,
975   háliȝ under heofenum,   ahafen purde;
ond þæs Iudeum   ȝnornsorȝa mæst,
perum pansæliȝum   pyrda laðost—
þær hie hit for porulde   pendan meahton—
cristenra ȝefean.   Ða sio cpen bebead
980   ofer eorlmæȝen   aras fysan
ricene to rade,   sceoldon Rómparena
ofer heanne holm   hlaford secean
ond þam piȝȝende   pilspella mæst
seolfum ȝesecȝan   þ[æt]ðæt siȝorbeacen
985   þurh meotodes est   meted pære,
funden in foldan   þæt ær feala mæla
behyded pæs   halȝum to teonan,
cristenum folce;   þa ðam cininȝe pearð
þurh þa mæran pord   mod ȝeblissod,
990   ferhð ȝefeonde;   næs þa fricȝendra

(971) *boden*] *bodan. fæðmað*] *fæðmeð.* (972) *rod* not in the MS. (974)
siȝe becna with *a* above the line and a tag. (984) *þæt*] *þe.* (989) Maier
read *mód* but the mark is apparently the tail of the letter above.

(974-5) Note the sg. verb after 'þara þe'; cp 970, 1288; Grossmann,
Das ags. Relativ 56-61; Bauch, *op.cit.* 54-7.
(978) Possibly 'if only they could alter it!' Cp Cosijn, *Aanteekeningen
op den Beowulf* 32. Or read *þæt . . . ne meahton* as suggested by Grein.

under ʒoldhoman   ʒád in burʒum,
feorran ʒeferede;   pæs him frofra mæst,
ʒeporden in porlde   æt ðam pillspelle,
hlihende hyʒe,   þe him hererǽspan
995   ofer eastpeʒas,   aras brohton
hu ʒesundne sið   ofer s[p]onrade
secʒas mid siʒecpen   asete[d] hæfdon
on Creca land;   hie se casere heht
ofstum myclum   eft ʒearpian
1000   sylfe to siðe;   secʒas ne ʒældon
syððan andspare   edre ʒehyrdon,
æðelinʒes pord.   Heht he Elenan hǽl
abeodan, beadurofre   ʒif hie brim nesen,
7 ʒesundne sið   settan mosten,
1005   hæleð hpætmode   to þære halʒan byriʒ.
Heht hire þa aras   eac ʒebeodan,
Constantinus   þæt hio cirican þær
on þam beorhhliðe   beʒra rædum
ʒetimbrede,   tempel dryhtnes
1010   on Caluarie   Criste to pillan,
hæleðum to helpe   þær sio haliʒe ród
ʒemeted pæs,   mærost beama
þara þe ʒefruʒnen   foldbuende
on eorðpeʒe;   hio ʒeefnde spa
1015   siððan pinemaʒas   pestan brohton
ofer laʒufæsten   leofspell maniʒ.
Ða seo cpen bebead   cræftum ʒetyde
sundor asecean,   þa selestan,
þa þe prætlicost   pyrcan cuðon
1020   stanʒefoʒum,   on þam stedepanʒe
ʒirpan Ʒodes tempel   spa hire ʒasta peard
reord of roderum;   heo þa rode heht
ʒolde bepeorcean   7 ʒimcynnum,   fol. 131ᵃ
mid þam æðelestum   eorcnanstanum,

---

(996) *sponrade*] *spon rade*. (997) *aseted*] *aseten*. (1019) The *n* of *cuðon* above the line and a tag.

(1003b) nesen: for the pret. subj. see Prollius, *op.cit.* 19.

1025 besett[a]n searocræftum 7 þa in seolfren fæt
    locum belucan þær þæt lifes treo,
    selest siȝebeama siððan punode
    æðel[e], [u]nbrȩce; þær bið a ȝearu
    praðu pannhalum pita ȝehpylces,
1030 sæce 7 sorȝe; hie sona þær
    þurh þa halȝan ȝesceaft helpe findaþ,
    ȝodcunde ȝife. Spylce Iudas onfenȝ
    æfter fyrstmearce fulpihtes bæð
    7 ȝeclænsod pearð Criste ȝetrype,
1035 lifpearde leof; his ȝeleafa pearð
    fæst on ferhðe siððan frofre ȝast
    píc ȝepunode in þæs peres breostum,
    bylde to bote; he þæt betere ȝeceas,
    puldres pynne 7 þam pyrsan piðsóc,
1040 deofulȝildum 7 ȝedpolan fylde,
    unrihte ǽ; him pearð ece cyninȝ,
    meotud milde, Ȝod, mihta pealdend:—

                    .xiii.

    þA pæs ȝefulpad se ðe ær feala tida
    leoht ȝearu...
1045 inbryrded breostsefa on þæt betere lif,
    ȝepended to puldre. Huru pyrd ȝescreaf
    þæt he spa ȝeleaffull 7 spa leof Ȝode
    in porldrice peorðan sceolde
    Criste ȝecpeme. þæt ȝecyðed pearð
1050 siððan Elene heht Eusebium
    on rædȝeþeaht, Rome bisceop
    ȝefetian on fultum, forðsnoterne,

(1025) *besettan*] Be setton. (1028) *æðele unbrȩce*] *æðelu anbrȩce*. (1041)
cyning] *rex*.

(1028a) For the emendation cp *J J J* 23. *æðele* is required by the masculine antecedent *siȝebeam*. The final *u* of the MS reading may be due to
anticipation but see note to 861. The MS *anbrȩce* is for *unbrȩce* 'inviolable'; it may be a scribal error or contain the negative *on-*. For half-
lines made up of two adjectives see Klaeber, *Anglia* xxviii. 440.

    hæleða ȝerædum   to þære halȝan byriȝ
    þæt he ȝesette   on sacerdhád,
1055 in Ierusalem,   Iudas þam folce
    to bisceope,   burȝum on innan,
    þurh Ȝastes ȝife   to Ȝodes temple,
    cræftum ȝecorene,   7 hine Cyriacus
    þurh snyttro ȝeþeaht   syððan nemde
1060 nipan stefne;   nama þæs ȝecyrred
    beornes in burȝum   on þæt betere forð,
    'ǽ hælendes'.   Þa ȝen Elenan þæs
    mód ȝemynde   ýmb þa mæran pyrd
    ȝeneahhe for þam næȝlum   þe ðæs nerȝendes
1065 fét þurhpodon   7 his folme spa some,
    mid þam on rode þæs   rodera pealdend
    ȝefæstnod, frea mihtiȝ;   be ðam friȝnan onȝan
    Cristenra cpen,   Cyriacus bæd
    þæt hire þa ȝina   ȝastes mihtum
1070 ymb pundorpyrd   pillan ȝefylde,
    onpriȝe puldorȝifum   7 þæt pord ácpæð,
    to þam bisceope   bald reordode,
    'Þu me, eorla hleo,   þone æðelan beam,
    róde rodercininȝ[es]   ryhte ȝetæhtesð   fol. 131ᵇ
1075 on þa áhanȝen þæs   hæðenum folmum
    ȝasta ȝeocend,   Ȝodes aȝen bearn,
    neriȝend fira;   mec þæra næȝla ȝén
    on fyrhðsefan   fyrpet mynȝaþ;
    polde ic þæt ðu funde   þa ðe in foldan ȝén
1080 deope bedolfen   dierne sindon,
    heolstre behyded;   á min hiȝe sorȝað,
    reoniȝ reoteð   7 ȝeresteð no
    ærþan me ȝefylle   fæder ælmihtiȝ,
    pereda pealdend,   pillan minne,
1085 niða nerȝend   þurh þara næȝla cyme

(1074) *rodercininȝes*] *rodera cininȝ*/. Cp PBB x. 518.

(1053) For *ȝerædum* see *JJJ* 39–40.

(1074a) The erroneous assumption that 'eorla hleo' referred to God
may have given rise to the corruption in the text. The phrase would
then be parallel to 'rodera cininȝ'. *Róde* should perhaps be omitted.

haliʒ of hiehða.   Nu ðu hrædlice
eallum eaðmedum,   ar selesta,
þine bene onsend   in ða beorhtan ʒesceaft,
on puldres pyn,   bide piʒena þrym
1090 þæt þe ʒecyðe   cyninʒ ælmihtiʒ
hord under hrusan   þæt ʒehyded ʒén
duʒuðum dyrne   deoʒol bideð'.
þa se halʒa onʒan   hyʒe staðolian,
breostum onbryrded   bisceop þæs folces,
1095 ʒlædmód eode   ʒumena þreate
Ʒod herʒendra,   7 þa ʒeornlice
Cyriacus   on Caluarię
hleor onhylde,   hyʒerune ne mað,
Ʒastes mihtum   to Ʒode cleopode
1100 eallum eaðmedum,   bæd him enʒla peard
ʒeopeniʒean   uncuðe pyrd
nipan on nearpe   hpær he þara næʒla spiðost
on þam panʒstede   penan þorfte.
Leort ða tacen forð   þær hie to sæʒon
1105 fæder, frofre ʒast,   ðurh fyres bleo
up eðiʒean   þær þa æðelestan
hæleða ʒerædum   hydde pæron,
þurh nearusearpe,   næʒlas on eorðan.
Ða cpom semninʒa   sunnan beorhtra
1110 lacende liʒ;   leode ʒesapon
hira pillʒifan   pundor cyðan
ða ðær of heolstre   spylce heofonsteorran
oððe ʒodʒimmas   ʒrunde ʒetenʒe,
næʒlas of nearpe   neoðan scinende
1115 leohte lixton;   leode ʒefæʒon,
peorud pillhreðiʒ,   sæʒdon puldor Ʒode

(1104) A capital *L* erased before *Leort*. (1116) A mark over the *r* of
hreðig but it differs in shape from the usual accent.

(1106a) Sievers, *Anglia* i. 578 read *siðiʒean* but the MS reading makes
passable sense.

(1113a) Many editors emend to *ʒoldʒimmas* on account of Latin
'tamquam aurum fulgens in terra'. But *ʒodʒimmas* 'divine jewels',
'heavenly bodies' (cp Tolkien, *Medium Aevum* iii. 104–5) is in keeping
with *heofonsteorran* in 1112.

ealle ánmode þeah hie ær pæron
þurh deofles spild in ȝedþolan lanȝe,
acyrred fram Criste; hie cpædon þus,

1120 'Nu þe seolfe ȝeseoð siȝores tacen,
soðpundor Ȝodes þeah þe piðsocun ǽr
mid leasinȝum. Nu is in leoht cymen,
onþriȝen þyrda biȝanȝ; puldor þæs aȝe
on heannesse heofonrices Ȝod.'

1125 Ða þæs ȝeblissod se ðe to bote ȝehþearf
þurh bearn Ȝodes, bisceop þara leoda
nipan stefne; he þan næȝlan onfenȝ
eȝesan ȝeáclod 7 þære arpyrðan
cpene brohte; hæfde Ciriacus

1130 eall ȝefylled spa him seo æðele bebead,
pifes pillan; þa þæs popes hrinȝ,
hat heafodpylm, ofer hleor ȝoten;
nalles for torne tearas feollon
ofer þira ȝesþon; puldre [i]s ȝefylled

1135 cpene pilla; heo on cneop sette
leohte ȝeleafan, lác peorðode
blissum hremiȝ þe hire brunȝen þæs
ȝnyrna to ȝeoce; Ȝode þancode,   fol. 132ª

(1120) The last two letters of *seolfe* on an erasure. (1134) *puldre is*]
puldres.

(1131b) Cp *Guth.* 1339; *Crist* 537; *Andreas* 1278. Some editors have
supposed that the kenning meant 'globe of weeping', 'tear'; cp Kock,
JJJ 5–6; *Anglia* xliv. 106. This view has in its favour the apparent
parallelism of 'hat heafodpylm'. But it may mean 'circle (eye socket)
of weeping', when the conception is of hot tears overflowing like water
boiling over from a cauldron. *E(a)ȝhrinȝ* 'eye-socket' might suggest
such a kenning; cp Brooks, *English and Germanic Studies* ii. 68–74.
(1134a) þira ȝesþon: 'web of wires or filigree work'. Perhaps, as the
tears fell over St Helena's breast, a pendant ornamented with filigree
or gold thread. Cp *hrinȝa ȝesþon* (MS *ȝesþonȝ*) Gen. 377.
(1134b) If *þæs* is understood from 1131, *puldres* is either an unrecorded
adverb 'gloriously' or genitive after *ȝefylled*, 'fulfilled with glory'. Or
puldres could be a corruption of *puldr is*; cp *moncyn is=moncynnes*,
in Rypins, *Three Old English Prose Texts* (EETS 161) 67, 16; or, as we
have assumed, of *puldre is*; cp the parallel construction in 452. Translate 'the queen's will is fulfilled gloriously'.

siʒora dryhtne   þæs þe hio soð ʒecneop
1140 andpeardlice   þæt pæs oft bodod
feor ær beforan   fram fruman porulde
folcum to frofre;   heo ʒefylled pæs
pisdomes ʒife   7 þa pic beheold
haliʒ heofonlic ʒast,   hreðer peardode,
1145 æðelne innoð;   spa hie ælmihtiʒ,
siʒebearn Ჳodes,   sioððan freoðode. 7

.xiiii.

ONʒan þa ʒeornlice   ʒastʒerynum
on sefan secean soðfæstnesse,
peʒ to puldre;   huru peorda Ჳod
1150 ʒefullæste,   fæder on roderum,
cininʒ ælmihtiʒ,   þæt seo cpen beʒeat
pillan in porulde;   pæs se pitedóm
þurh fyrnpitan   beforan sunʒen
eall æfter orde   spa hit eft ʒelamp
1155 ðinʒa ʒehpylces;   þeodcpen onʒan
þurh Ჳastes ʒife   ʒeorne secan,
nearpe ʒeneahhe   to hpan hio þa næʒlas selost
7 deorlicost   ʒedon meahte
duʒoðum to hroðer,   hpæt þæs pære dryhtnes pilla.
1160 Heht ða ʒefetiʒean   forðsnotterne
ricene to rune,   þone þe rædʒeþeaht
þurh ʒleape miht   ʒeorne cuðe,
frodne on ferhðe   7 hine friʒnan onʒan
hpæt him þæs on sefan   selost þuhte
1165 to ʒelæstenne   7 his lare ʒeceas
þurh þeodscipe;   he hire [þriste] oncpæð,
'Þæt is ʒedafenlic   þæt ðu dryhtnes pord
on hyʒe healde,   haliʒe rune,
cpen selest[e],   7 þæs cininʒes bebod

(1166) *þriste* not in MS. (1169) *seleste*] selest.

(1149b) Editors read *we(o)ro/uda* but cp Sievers-Brunner §159 n. 8.

1170 ȝeorne beȝanȝe   nu þe Ȝod sealde
saple siȝesped   7 snyttro cræft,
neriȝend fira;   þu ðas næȝlas hat
þam æðelestan   eorðcyninȝa,
burȝaȝendra,   on his bridels dón
1175 meare to midlum;   þæt maniȝum sceall
ȝeond middanȝeard   mære peorðan
þonne æt sæcce mid þy   oferspiðan mæȝe
feonda ȝehþylcne   þonne fyrdhþate
on tpa healfe   tohtan secaþ,
1180 speordȝeniðlan   þær hie [siȝor] pillað,
prað pið praðum.   He ah æt piȝȝe sped,
siȝor æt sæcce   7 sybbe ȝehþær,
æt ȝefeohte frið   se ðe fo[r]an lædeð
bridels on blancan   þonne beadurofe
1185 æt ȝárþræce,   ȝuman ȝecoste
berað bord 7 ord;   þis bið beorna ȝehþam
pið æȝlæce   unoferspiðed
pæpen æt piȝȝe   be ðam se pitȝa sanȝ
snottor searuþancum—   sefa deop ȝepód,
1190 pisdomes ȝepitt—   he þæt pord ȝecpæð,
"Cuþ þæt ȝepyrðeð   þæt þæs cyninȝes sceal
mearh under modeȝum   midlum ȝepeorðod,
bridelshrinȝum;   bið þæt beacen Ȝode
haliȝ nemned   7 se hpæteadiȝ
1195 piȝȝe peorðod   se þæt picȝ byr[e]ð" '.
Þa þæt ofstlice   eall ȝelæste   fol. 132ᵇ
Elene for eorlum,   æðelinȝes heht,

(1180) *sigor*] *ymb.* (1183) *foran*] *fonan.* (1189) A letter erased after *deop.* (1195) *byreð*] *byrð.*

(1177) A subj. after *þonne* is unusual but here may indicate the subjective content of the clause; see Prollius, *Über den syntact. Gebrauch des Conjunctivs* 27.
(1180) The MS reading *ymb* may conceal a word with an initial *s* such as *sinc*; cp *Beowulf* 1204. Many editors read *ymb siȝe* (*siȝor*) *pinnað.*
(1188b) Zechariah xiv, 20.
(1195b) Note *se* for *þone*; cp *Genesis* 2119; Grossmann, *op.cit.* 34. The metre requires *byreð.*

 beorna beaȝȝifan, bridels frætpan,
 hire selfre suna sende to lace
1200 ofer ȝeofenes stream ȝife unscynde.
 Heht þa tosomne þa heo seleste
 mid Iudeum ȝumena piste,
 hæleða cynnes, to þære halȝan byriȝ
 cuman in þa ceastre; þa seo cpen onȝan
1205 læran leofra heap þæt hie lufan dryhtnes
 7 sybbe spa same sylfra betþeonum,
 freondræddenne fæste ȝelæston,
 leahtorlease in hira lifes tíd
 ond þæs latteopes larum hyrdon
1210 cristenum þeapum þe him Cyriacus
 bude, boca ȝleap; pæs se bissceophad
 fæȝere befæsted; oft him feorran to
 laman, limseoce, lefe cpomon,
 healte, heorudreoriȝe, hreofe 7 blinde,
1215 heane, hyȝeȝeomre; symle hælo þær
 æt þam bisceope, bote fundon,
 ece to aldre. Ða ȝén him Elene forȝeaf
 sincpeorðunȝa þa hio pæs siðes fus
 eft to eðle 7 þa eallum bebead
1220 on þam ȝumrice Ꝩod herȝendum,
 perum 7 pifum, þæt hie peorðeden
 mode 7 mæȝene þone mæran dæȝ,
 heortan ȝehiȝdum, in ðam sio haliȝe ród
 ȝemeted pæs, mærost beama
1225 þara þe of eorðan up ápeoxe,
 ȝeloden under leafum; pæs þa lencten aȝan
 butan syx nihtum ær sumeres cyme
 on Mai[u]s monað; sie þara manna ȝehpam
 behliden helle duru, heofones ontyned,

(1228) *Maius monað*] *maias.kl.*.

___

(1228a) The abbreviation must be expanded to *kalend* 'month' not
kalendas as *Maias* suggests. The kalends of May fall in the second half
of April and the reading *kalendas* is, therefore, appropriate neither for
the festival of the Invention on May 3, nor for the beginning of summer
on May 9. For the reading in the text see Sisam, *Studies* 14.

1230 ece ʒeopenad   enʒla rice,
      dream unhpilen   7 hira dæl scired
      mid Marian   þe on ʒemynd nime
      þære deorestan   dæʒpeorðunʒa,
      rode under roderum   þa se ricesða,
1235 ealles oferpealdend,   earme beþeahte.   finit:—

                    .xv.

     ÞUS ic fród 7 fús,   þurh þæt fæcne hus,
     pordcræft pæf   7 pundrum læs,
     þraʒum þreodude   7 ʒeþanc reodode,
     nihtes nearpe;   nysse ic ʒearpe,
1240 be ðære [rode] riht   ær me rumran ʒeþeaht,
     þurh ða mæran miht,   on modes þeaht,
     pisdóm onpreah;   ic pæs peorcum fáh,
     synnum asæled,   sorʒum ʒepæled,
     bitrum ʒebunden,   bisʒum beþrunʒen,
1245 ær me lare onlaʒ   þurh leohtne had,

(1240) *rode* not in MS. (1241) The *þ* of *þeaht* added later. (1244)
bisʒum] *besʒum* with an *i* added above the line.

_____

(1232) For the subjunctive cp Prollius, *op.cit.* 11.
(1236b) Cp 880. *Hus* is a metaphor for the poet's body comparable to
feorʒbold, feorhhus. *Fæcne* either means 'deceitful' or is an example of the
otherwise unique sense 'old'. See BTS, s.v. *fæcne*. *þurh* means either
'because of' or 'by means of'.
(1237a) Most editors emend to *pordcræftum* for the metre.
(1238b) The rhyme supports the unique *reodode*. The supposition
that it is a variant of *hridrian* 'sift' is supported by the use of a similar
metaphor in Otfrid (*Evangelienbuch* iv. 13, 16), where it expresses the
sifting image of Luke xxii, 31: 'thaz muast er redan iu thaz muat, so
man korn in sibe duat': see Grein-Köhler, s.v. *reodian*. The absence of
the second *r* may be due either to the influence of *hriðian* or to the
rhyme.
(1240a) Grein's emendation.
(1243a) The image is from Proverbs v, 22. Cp Menner, *Sol. & Sat.*
132–3.
(1244a) The rhyme supports the hapax *bitrum*; cp Klaeber, ESt lv.
284; Ekwall, Anglia Beibl xxxiii. 65.
(1245b) 'gloriously'; cp *Beo.* 1335.

F   71

ʒamelum to ʒeoce,   ʒife unscynde
mæʒencyninʒ ámæt   7 on ʒemynd beʒeat,
torht ontynde,   tidum ʒerymde,
báncofan onband,   breostlocan onpand,
1250 leoðucræft onleac   þæs ic lustum breac,
pillum in porlde;   ic þæs puldres treopes
oft nales æne   hæfde inʒemynd
ær ic þæt pundor   onpriʒen hæfde,   fol. 133ᵃ
ymb þone beorhtan beam   spa ic on bocum fand,
1255 pyrda ʒanʒum,   on ʒepritum cyðan
be ðam siʒebeacne.   A pæs sæc[ʒ] oð ðæt
cnyssed cearpelmum,   ᚻ. drusende
þeah he in medohealle   maðmas þeʒe,
æplede ʒold . ᛗ . ʒnornode,

(1256) *sæcʒ*] *sæcc*.

(1247b) The rhyme suggests that *beʒeat* is from *beʒietan* but derivation from *beʒeotan* makes better sense.

(1249) Cp 86b. (1250) Cp 522.

(1256b) Most editors read *secʒ*. For *sæcʒ* see Introduction p. 12; but *sæcc* may be for *sec*; cp *Andreas* 1225; *Waldere* 1. 5; *Beo.* 2863.

(1257b) The c-rune usually stands for *cen* 'torch'; see *Rune Poem* 16–18. 'Cen drusende' would mean 'dying torch'. There is a comparable image in *Bibliothek der ags. Prosa* iii. 148: 'Spa hpilc man spa sæʒð leasunʒa on his nehstan, his leohtfet bið acpænced on ðam ytemestan dæʒe'. In both passages the life of man is compared to a torch or lamp. The interpretation *cyn* (Trautmann, BB i. 70) and also *cene* (Kemble *Archaeologia* xxviii, 363) have been supported by reference to *Crist* 797, but although the partial spellings in Riddle 65 might be compared it is more probable that in *Crist* the first three runes together spell *cyn* 'mankind'. Cp Riddle 20. But some support for the interpretation *cene* might be seen in the spelling *cæn* in St John's College 17 and in the Welsh gloss *guichr* 'anger', 'impetuous' in MS Bodley Auct. F. 4. 32 (cp Derolez p. 159). Or *cen* might have been taken to equal *cyn* as *wen* equals *wyn*.

(1259a) Usually interpreted 'embossed gold', since *æppel* means any spherical object, such as an eyeball, as well as 'apple'. Embossed gold would presumably refer to objects with embossed work such as can be seen on the Sutton Hoo helmet. Cp R. Woolf, *Juliana* p. 87. But ON *apalgrár*, Germ. *apfelgrau* etc (cp NED *Dapple-grey*) suggest that *æpled* might mean 'circular' as well as 'spherical'. The semantic development seems to have occurred, also, in French *gris-pommelé*. 'The

1260 ·ᚷ· ᵹefera nearusorᵹe dreah,
enᵹe rune þær him. ᛗ. fore
milpaðas mæt, modiᵹ þræᵹde,
pirum ᵹeplenced. ᚹ . is ᵹespiðrad,
ᵹomen æfter ᵹearum, ᵹeoᵹoð is ᵹecyrred,
1265 ald onmedla. ᚻ . þæs ᵹeara
ᵹeoᵹoðhades ᵹlæm; nu synt ᵹeardaᵹas
æfter fyrstmearce forð ᵹepitene,
lífpynne ᵹeliden spa. �|.toᵹlideð,

(1263) The p-rune has been written twice and the first one erased.
(1268) An erasure before the l-rune.

---

rounded gold' may have been used in contrast with the 'twisted gold'
either to mean coins, such as the *solidi* which were common in the
Islands of Bornholm, Öland and Götland, Zealand and Funen during
the Migration Period; or the phrase might refer to some circular object
such as a ring, armlet or torque, or an annular or saucer brooch, or to
the bars of gold which were made into rings and used like the 'twisted
gold' as currency. Cp Shetelig and Falk, *Scandinavian Archaeology*,
trans. E. V. Gordon, 230 f. The y-rune is usually *yr* 'bow'; see *Rune
Poem* 84–6. But it may, also, be 'horn' as suggested by Holthausen in
Anglia xxxv. 175–7 which would fit well in *Fates* 103. For the view
that the runes are only names see Sisam, *Studies* 21–8; cp Elliott, *English
Studies* xxvii. 53.

(1260a) 'an inevitable companion'; cp Bede's *Death Song neidfaeru*
'inevitable journey'. The n-rune stands for *nyd* 'necessity'.

(1261a) Perhaps a pun: 'oppressive secret' and 'narrow rune'.

(1261b) The e-rune stands for *eoh* 'horse'.

(1263b) The p-rune stands for *pyn* 'joy'; cp Sievers, *Anglia* xiii. 3–4.

(1265b) The u-rune usually stands for *ur* 'aurochs', 'bison'; see *Rune
Poem* 4–6. Kemble, *op.cit.* 363, suggested *ur* 'of old'; Cosijn, *Verslagen en
Mededeelingen der Konink. Akademie van Wetenschappen van Amsterdam*
(Afd. Letterkunde 3rd ser.) vii. 56–7, Gollancz, *Cynewulf's Christ* 181–2,
Sisam, *op.cit.* 27, all suggest *ur(e)* 'our'. This has been supported by the
gloss *noster* in Cott. Dom. A ix but the Latin glosses in this MS are
probably the work of an Elizabethan antiquary; see Hempl, MPh i.
135–41; Sisam, *op.cit.* 18. The context and parallelism require a meaning
'wealth' perhaps related to Latin *aurum* PG. **urom* as suggested by
Sievers (*Anglia* xiii. 7); cp Norwegian *Rune Poem* 2–3 for *ur* 'dross'. Or
ur 'bison' might have been thought to have the double sense of *feoh*.
This interpretation has at least the advantage of fitting *Fates* 101 and
Crist 805, also.

(1268b) The l-rune is *lagu* 'water' Cp *swa lagu toglideþ*, Vercelli
Homily X f. 70.

flodas ȝefysde. ᚠ . æȝhpam biδ
1270 læne under lyfte;   landes frætpe,
        ȝepitaþ under polcnum   pinde ȝeliccost
        þonne he for hæleδum   hlud astiȝeδ,
        pæδeδ be polcnum,   pedende færeδ,
        7 eft semninȝa   spiȝe ȝepyrδeδ
1275 in nedcleofan   nearpe ȝeheaδrod,
        þream forþrycced;   spa þeos por[u]ld
        eall ȝepiteδ
        7 eac spa some   þe hire on purdon
        atydrede   tionleȝ nimeδ,
1280 δonne Dryhten sylf   dom ȝeseceδ
        enȝla peorude;   sceall æȝhpylc δær
        reordberendra   riht ȝehyran
        dæda ȝehpylcra   þurh þæs Deman muδ
        7 porda spa same,   ped ȝesyllan
1285 eallra unsnyttro   ær ȝesprecenra,
        þristra ȝeþonca.   þonne on þreo dæleδ
        in fyres fenȝ   folc anra ȝehpylc
        þara þe ȝepurdon   on pidan feore
        ofer sidne ȝrund;   soδfæste bioδ
1290 yfemest in þam ade,   eadiȝra ȝedryht,
        duȝuδ domȝeorne;   spa hie adreoȝan maȝon
        7 butan earfeδum   eaδe ȝeþolian,
        modiȝra mæȝen.   Him ȝemetȝaþ eall
        e[lδ]es leoma   spa him eδost biδ,
1295 sylfum ȝeseftost;   synfulle beoδ,
        mane ȝemenȝde,   in δam midle þread,
        hæleδ hiȝeȝeomre,   in hatne pylm,
        þrosme beþehte.   Biδ se þridda dæl,
        apyrȝede pomsceaδan,   in þæs pylmes ȝrund,
1300 lease leodhatan,   liȝe befæsted,
        þurh ærȝepyrht,   arleasra sceolu,

(1276) *poruld*] *porld*. (1294) *elδes*] *eδles*.

(1269b) The f-rune is *feoh* 'property'.
(1276b) For the emendation cp *Phoenix* 501.
(1294a) Zupitza reads *eldes*; Holthausen *ældes*. Cp Introduction p. 112

in ʒleda ʒripe.   Ᵹode no syððan
of ðam morðorhofe   in ʒemynd cumað,
puldorcyninʒe   ac hie porpene beoð
1305 of ðam heaðupylme   in helle ʒrund,
tornʒeniðlan.   Bið þam tpam dælum
unʒelice;   moton enʒla frean
ʒeseon, siʒora ʒod;   hie asodene beoð,
asundrod fram synnum   spa smæte ʒold
1310 þæt in pylme bið   pomma ʒehpylces,
þurh ofnes fýr,   eall ʒeclænsod,
amered 7 ʒemylted;   spa bið þara manna ælc fol. 133^b
ascyred 7 asceaden   scylda ʒehpylcre,
deopra firena,   þurh þæs domes fýr.
1315 Moton þonne siðþan   sybbe brucan,
eces eadpelan;   him bið enʒla peard
milde 7 bliðe   þæs ðe hie mána ʒehpylc
forsapon, synna peorc   7 to suna metudes
pordum cleopodon;   forðan hie nu on plite scinaþ
1320 enʒlum ʒelice,   yrfes brucaþ,
puldorcyninʒes   to pidan feore.   aMeN:—

(1309b) Cp Proverbs xvii, 3. The image is a commonplace in patristic
writings.

BIBLIOGRAPHY

I. BIBLIOGRAPHICAL LISTS

1908 K. Jansen, *Die Cynewulf-Forschung von ihren Anfängen bis zur Gegenwart*, BB xxiv.

1911 T. Schmitz, Die Cynewulf-Forschung 1908 u. 1909, Anglia Beibl xxii. 337–41.

1932 G. P. Krapp, *The Vercelli Book* (Anglo-Saxon Poetic Records), lxxxi–xciv.

1936 F. Holthausen, *Cynewulfs 'Elene'*, ix–xix.

II. LEXICONS

1899 R. Simons, *Cynewulfs Wortschatz*, BB iii.

III. MANUSCRIPT

1844 *The Quarterly Review* lxxv. 398–9.

1882 R. P. Wülcker, *Über das Vercellibuch*, Anglia, v. 451–65.

1888 A. S. Cook, *Cardinal Guala and the Vercelli Book*, University of California Library Bulletin 10.

1889 A. S. Cook, *Supplementary Note to* 'Cardinal Guala and the Vercelli Book', MLN iv. 212–13.

1889 A. S. Napier, *Collation der ae. Gedichte im Vercellibuch*, ZfdA xxxiii. 66–73.

1894 R. P. Wülcker, *Codex Vercellensis; die angelsächsische Handschrift zu Vercelli in getreuer Nachbildung.*

1906 W. Keller, *Angelsächsische Palaeographie*, Palaestra xliii.

1906 G. P. Krapp, *Andreas and the Fates of the Apostles*, ix–xx.

1913 M. Förster, *Il Codice Vercellese con Omelie e Poesie in Lingua Anglosassone.*

1913 M. Förster, *Der Vercelli-Codex 117 nebst Abdruck einiger altenglischer Homilien der Handschrift*, Studien zur englischen Philologie l.

1932 G. P. Krapp, *The Vercelli Book*, xi–lxxx.

1935 S. J. Herben, *The Vercelli Book: A New Hypothesis*, Speculum, x. 91–4.

1950 N. R. Ker, *Maier's Transcript of the Vercelli Book*, Medium Aevum xix. 17–25.

1953 K. Sisam, *Studies in the History of Old English Literature.*

IV. EDITIONS

1835? B. Thorpe, Appendix B to Mr Cooper's Report on Rymer's *Foedera.*

1840 J. Grimm, *Andreas und Elene.*

BIBLIOGRAPHY

1850 L. Ettmüller, *Engla and Seaxna Scôpas and Bôceras* (ll. 1–193 and Epilogue)
1856 J. M. Kemble, *Poetry of the Codex Vercellensis*.
1858 C. W. M. Grein, *Bibliothek der ags. Poesie* ii.
1877 J. Zupitza, *Elene* (1883, 1888, 1899).
1878 K. Koerner, *Einleitung in das Studium des ags.* (ll. 1–275).
1888 C. W. M. Grein and R. Wülcker, *Bibliothek der ags. Poesie* ii.
1905 F. Holthausen, *Cynewulfs 'Elene'* (1910, 1914, 1936).
1919 A. S. Cook, *Elene, Phoenix and Physiologus*.
1922 W. J. Sedgefield, *An Anglo-Saxon Verse Book* (ll. 1236–76).
1932 G. P. Krapp, *The Vercelli Book*.
1946 H. Sweet, *An Anglo-Saxon Reader*, rev. C. T. Onions (Epilogue) (1948, 1950, 1954).

IV. LANGUAGE

1884 J. Schürmann, *Darstellung der Syntax in Cynewulfs 'Elene'*.
1887 H. Leiding, *Die Sprache der Cynewulf'schen Dichtungen Crist, Juliana u. Elene.*
1888 M. Prollius, *Über den syntactischen Gebrauch des Conjunctivs in den Cynewulf'schen Dichtungen Elene, Juliana u. Crist.*
1906 H. Dunkhase, *Die Sprache der Wulfstan'schen Homilien in Wulfgeats Handschriften.*
1907 J. Weightman, *The Language and Dialect of the later Old English Poetry* (Liverpool Diss.).
1912 H. Bauch, *Die Kongruenz in der ags. Poesie.*
1912 W. Sorg, *Zur Syntax u. Stilistik des Pronominalgebrauches in der älteren ags. Dichtung.*
1914 W. Schlemilch, *Beiträge zur Sprache u. Orthographie Spätaltengl. Sprachdenkmäler der Übergangzeit*, Studien zur englischen Philologie xxxiv.

V. BACKGROUND AND SOURCES

For texts of the Invention of the Cross see Introduction.

1888 L.-J. Tixeront, *Les Origines de l'Église d'Édesse*, 163–75.
1889 E. Nestle, *De Sancta Cruce.*
1890 W. Deering, *The Anglosaxon Poets on the Judgement Day.*
1893 A. S. Cook, *The Date of the Old English 'Elene'*, Anglia xv. 9–20.
1894 V. Ryssel, *Syrische Quellen abendländischer Erzählungsstoffe*, Archiv xciii. 1–22.
1903 C. F. Brown, *Cynewulf and Alcuin*, MLA xviii. 308–34.
1904 W. O. Stevens, *The Cross in the Life and Literature of the Anglo-Saxons*, Yale Studies in English, xxiii.
1905 F. Holthausen, *Zur Quelle von Cynewulfs 'Elene'*, ZfdPh xxxvii, 1–19.

1908 C. F. Brown, *Irish-Latin Influence in Cynewulfian Texts*, ESt xl. 1–29.

1908 G. A. H. Grau, *Quellen und Verwandtschaften der älteren germanischen Darstellungen des jüngsten Gerichtes*, Studien zur englischen Philologie xxxi.

1910 F. Holthausen, *Zur Quelle von Cynewulfs 'Elene'*, Archiv cxxv. 83–8.

1912 J. Straubinger, *Die Kreuzauffindungslegende*.

1943 M.-M. Dubois, *Les Éléments latins dans la Poésie religieuse de Cynewulf*.

VI. METRE

1885 E. Sievers, *Zur Rhythmik des germanischen Alliterations-verses*, PBB x. 209–314, 451–545.

1887 E. Sievers, *ib.*, PBB xii. 454–82.

1925 E. Sievers, *Zu Cynewulf*, Neusprachliche Studien; Festgabe für Karl Luick 60–81.

1925 A. Heusler, *Deutsche Versgeschichte* (Grundriss der germanischen Philologie 8, i).

1942 S. K. Das, *Cynewulf and the Cynewulf Canon*.

VII. AUTHORSHIP

1878 R. P. Wülcker, *Über den Dichter Cynewulf*, Anglia i, 483–507.

1891 E. Sievers, *Zu Cynewulf*, Anglia xiii. 1–25.

1932 K. Sisam, *Cynewulf and his Poetry*, Proceedings of the British Academy xviii.

1949 C. Schaar, *Critical Studies in the Cynewulf Group*, Lund Studies in English xvii.

VIII. RUNES

1840 J. M. Kemble, *On Anglo-Saxon Runes*, Archaeologia xxviii. 327–72.

1842 B. Thorpe, *Codex Exoniensis*, 50, 501–2.

1859 F. Dietrich, *review of Leo*, 'Quae de se ipso Cynewulfus... tradiderit', Jahrbuch f. romanische. u englische Literatur i. 242–3.

1869 M. Rieger, *Über Cynewulf*, ZfdPh i. 219–26.

1891 P. J. Cosijn, *Cynewulfs Runenverzen*, Verslagen en Mededeelingen der Konink. Akademie van Wetenschappen van Amsterdam (Afd. Letterkunde 3rd series) vii. 54–64.

1891 E. Sievers, *Zu Cynewulf*, Anglia xiii. 1–25.

1892 I. Gollancz, *Cynewulf's Christ*, 173–84.

1898 M. Trautmann, *Kynewulf der Bischof und Dichter*, BB i.

BIBLIOGRAPHY

1899 M. Trautmann, *Zu Cynewulfs Runenstellen*, BB ii.

1900 A. S. Cook, *The Christ of Cynewulf*, 151–63.

1901 A. J. Barnouw, *Die Runenstelle der Himmelfahrt*, Archiv cvii. 382–5.

1903 G. Hempl, *Hickes's Additions to the Runic Poem*, MPh i. 135–41.

1911 F. Holthausen, *Zu den altenglischen Rätseln*, Anglia xxxv, 175–7.

1912 F. Tupper, *The Cynewulfian Runes of the Religious Poems*, MLN xxvii. 131–7.

1932–3 C. L. Wrenn, *Late Old English Rune Names*, Medium Aevum i. 24–34, ii. (*corrigenda*), and C. E. Wright, A Postscript to 'Late Old English Rune Names', Medium Aevum v. 149–51, 1936.

1932 K. Sisam, *Cynewulf and his Poetry*, Proceedings of the British Academy xviii.

1953 R. W. V. Elliott, Cynewulf's Runes in *Elene* and *Crist*, English Studies xxxiv.

1954 R. Derolez, *Runica Manuscripta*.

IX. TEXTUAL CRITICISM

1869 M. Rieger, *Über Cynewulf*, ZfdPh i. 215–26, 313–34.

1878 E. Sievers, *review of Zupitza's 'Elene'*, Anglia i. 573–81.

1879 K. Körner, *ib.*, ESt ii. 252–62.

1879 B. ten Brink, *ib.*, AnzfdA v. 53–70.

1881 P. J. Cosijn, *Anglosaxonica*, Tijdschrift voor Nederlandsche Taal- en Letterkunde i. 143–8.

1882 E. Sievers, *review of Körner's 'Einleitung'*, Gott. gel. Anz. 993–1001.

1883 P. Lefèvre, *Das altenglische Gedicht vom heiligen Guthlac*, Anglia vi. 181–240.

1884 F. Kluge, *review of Zupitza's 'Elene'*, Literaturblatt, v. 138–9.

1901 F. Holthausen, *Zu alt. u. mittelenglischen Dichtungen*, Anglia xxiii. 516.

1904 F. Holthausen, *Zu Cynewulfs 'Elene'*, Anglia Beibl xv. 73–4.

1906 R. Imelmann, *review of Holthausen's 'Elene'*, Anglia Beibl xvii. 225–6.

1906 F. Holthausen, *Zur altenglischen Literatur*, Anglia Beibl xvii. 176–8.

1906 F. Klaeber, *Notizen zu Cynewulfs 'Elene'*, Anglia xxix. 271–2.

1907 F. Holthausen, *Zur altenglischen Literatur*, Anglia Beibl xviii. 77–8, 201–8.

1907 M. Trautmann, *Berichtigungen, Erklärungen u. Vermutungen zu Cynewulfs Werken*, BB xxiii.

1908 J. v. d. Warth, *Metrisch-Sprachliches u. Textkritisches zu Cynewulfs Werken*.

1912 J. W. Bright, *An Idiom of the Comparative in Anglo-Saxon*, MLN xxvii. 181–3.

1912 E. A. Kock, *review of Holthausen's* 'Elene', ESt xliv. 392–5.

1917 F. Holthausen, *Zu altenglischen Denkmälern*, ESt li. 183–4.

1918 E. A. Kock, *Jubilee Jaunts and Jottings*, Lunds Universitets Aarskrift (N.S. Pt. i) xiv(2).

1919 F. Klaeber, *Concerning the Functions of Old English* 'Geweorðan', JEGPh xviii. 250–71.

1919 E. A. Kock, *Interpretations and Emendations of Early English Texts*, Anglia xliii. 298–312.

1920 E. A. Kock, *ib.*, Anglia xliv. 245–60.

1920 J. H. G. Grattan, *review of Cook's* 'Elene, Phoenix and Physiologus', MLR xv. 177–8.

1921 F. Klaeber, *ib.*, ESt lv. 280–5.

1921 F. Holthausen, *Zu altenglischen Gedichten*, Anglia Beibl xxxii. 136–8.

1922 E. Ekwall, *review* of Cook's 'Elene etc', Anglia Beibl xxxiii. 61–7.

1922 E. A. Kock, *Plain Points and Puzzles*, Lunds Universitets Aarskrift (N.S. Pt. i) xvii.

1923 E. A. Kock, *Interpretations and Emendations of Early English Texts*, Anglia xlvii. 264–73.

1924 F. Holthausen, *Zu altenglischen Dichtungen*, Anglia Beibl, xxxv. 276–7.

1946 O. Arngart, *Some Notes on Cynewulf's* 'Elene', English Studies xxvii. 19–21.

1946 K. Sisam, *Notes on Old English Poetry*, RES xxii. 257–68.

GLOSSARY

In the glossary words will be found under the forms in which they occur in the text, except that nouns and adjectives will be found under the *nom.sg.* and verbs under the infinitive (except that the present forms of 'to be' will be found under *beon*, the pret. forms under *pæs*); pronouns under the nom.sg.m. except the 1st and 2nd pers. of the personal pronouns which will be found under the nom.sg. or nom.pl. Irregular or variant grammatical and phonological forms have cross references to the words under which they are dealt with. References are to lines of the text and are selective only. Italicized references indicate an emendation. An *n* after a line reference indicates a note; a reference preceded by an asterisk a hypothetical form.

The order of the letters is alphabetical; but *æ* is treated as a separate letter after *a*; *þ*, *ð* after *t*. The OE characters *ȝ*, *p* are replaced by *g*, *w*. The prefix *ge-* is ignored in the arrangement of the glossary. Abbreviations are the commonly accepted ones (see *Deor*, ed. Kemp Malone, p. 32, or *Waldere*, ed. F. Norman, p. 49).

Reference is made to the *New English Dictionary* by printing the NED word (under which the OE word is discussed) in square brackets after the headword. No reference is made to the NED when the history of the headword is well-known or when the form in the NED is identical with the headword. Unless otherwise stated the NED reference is to the same part of speech as the headword.

A

ā, *adv.*, always 743, 801, 893.

ābannan, *v.(7)*, summon 34.

ābēodan, *v. (2)*, offer, announce 87, 1003.

ābrēotan, *v.(2)*, [+ BRET]; slay 510.

ac, *conj.*, but 222, 355, 450.

ācennan, *w.v.(1)*, [AKEN(NE)²]; give birth to 5.

ācīgan, *w.v.(1)*, call 603.

geāclian, *w.v.(2)*, frighten 57.

ācweðan, *v.(5)*, [+ QUETHE]; speak 1071.

ācyrran, *w.v.(1)*, [+ CHARE]; turn away 1119.

ād, *m.a-stem*, pyre, fire 585, 950, 1290.

ādrēogan, *v.(2)*, [ADREE]; endure 705

āfēdan, *w.v.(1)*, rear 913.

āfyrhtan, *w.v.(1)*, terrify 56.

āgalan, *v.(6)*, [+ GALE¹)]; chant 27.

āgan, *pret-pres.(7)*, [OWE], possess 356, 725, 1123, 1181.

āgān, *anom.v.*, depart 1226.

āgangan, *v.(7)*, pass 1.

āgen, *adj.*, own 179, 599.

āgifan, *v.(5)*, give 167, 455, 587.

āhebban, *v.(6)*, raise, rear 10, 17, 353, 837, 861, 867.

āhōn, *v.(7)*, [AHANG]; crucify 180, 210, 453, 475n.

āhȳðan, *w.v.(1)*, plunder 41.

al, *see* eal(l).

ald, *see* eald.

aldor, *m.a-stem*, [ALDER²]; prince 97.

aldor, *n.a-stem*, life 132; **on aldre,** ever 571; **to aldre,** for ever 349.

aldordōm, *m.a-stem*, authority 767

ālesan, *v.(5)*, [LEASE¹]; select 286.

ālȳsan, *w.v.(1)*, [+ LEESE²]; redeem 181.

āmerian, *w.v.(1)*, [+ MERE¹]; purify 1312.

āmetan, *v.(5)*, mete out, measure 729, 1247.

ān, *num.adj. pron.*, one 417, 585; **ānra gehwylc**, each 1287.

anbid, *n.a-stem*, expectation 884n.

ānboren, *p.pt.*, only-begotten 392.

anda, *m.n-stem*, [AND(E)]; vexation 969.

andsǣc, *n.a-stem*, [ANDSECH]; opposition, denial 472.

andswaru, *f.ō-stem*, answer 166, 642.

andswerian, *w.v.(1)*, answer 396.

andweard, *adj.*, present 630.

andweardlīce, *adv.*, now present 1140.

andwlita, *m.n-stem*, [ANLETH]; face 298.

andwyrde, *n.ja-stem*, [ANDWURDE *v.*]; answer 545.

ānforlǣtan, *v.(7)*, relinquish 630, 946.

ānhaga, *m.n-stem*, solitary man 604.

ānhȳdig, *adj.*, resolute 828, 847.

ānmōd, *adj.*, [ANMOD]; unanimous 396.

*āpundrian, *w.v.(2)*, adjudge 580n.

ār, *f.ō-stem*, honour 308; **mid ārum**, ceremoniously 714.

ār, *m.a-stem*, messenger, 76, 737, 995, 1087.

ārǣran, *w.v.(1)*, [AREAR]; raise, elate 129, 803.

āreccan, *w.v.(1)*, [ARECCHE]; declare 635.

ārfæst, *adj.*, honourable, gracious 12, 512.

ārīsan, *v.(1)*, arise 187.

ārlēas, *adj.*, impious 835.

ārwyrðe, *adj.*, venerable 1128.

āsǣlan, *w.v.(1)*, [+ SEAL²]; bind 1243.

āscēadan, *v.(7)*, [+ SHADE²]; separate from, hold aloof 470, 1313.

āscyrian, *w.v.(1)*, separate 1313.

āsēcean, *w.v.(1)*, seek out 407, 1018.

āsēoðan, *v.(2)*, [+ SEETHE]; purify 1308.

āsettan, *w.v.(1)*, set down, accomplish 846, 862, 997.

āspyrigean, *w.v.(1)*, [+ SPEER¹]; discover 467.

āstīgan, *v.(1)*, [ASTY(E)]; rise 188, 794, 1272.

āsundrian, *w.v.(2)*, separate 1309.

ātȳdran, *w.v.(1)*, [+ TIDDER¹]; procreate 1279.

āþrēotan, *v.(2)*, irk 368.

āwa, *adv.*, always 950.

āweaxan, *v.(7)*, grow 1225.

āweccan, *w.v.(1)*, [AWECCHE]; awake, raise up 304, 781, 926.

āweorpan, *v.(3)*, [AWARP]; cast out, reject 762, 770.

āwer, *adv.*, anywhere 33.

āwrītan, *v.(1)*, write 91.

āwyrgan, *w.v.(1)*, [AWARIE]; curse 1299.

Æ

ǣ, *f.i-stem*, law 198.

ǣbylgþ, *f.ō-n.i-stem*, transgression 401 (cp Sievers-Brunner § 255. 3).

ǣclǣca, *m.n-stem*, [EGLECHE a.]; demon, wretch 901.

ǣclēaw, *see* **ǣglēaw**.

ǣcræft, *m.a-stem*, knowledge of the law, religion 435.

ǣfen, *n.ja-stem*, evening 139.

æfre, *adv.*, ever 349.

æfst, *mf.i-stem*, [EVEST]; envy 308, 496.

æfter, *prep.w.dat.*, after 233; concerning 675; along, through 135n, 971; for 827.

æghwā, *pron.*, each 1269.

æghwylc, *pron.*, each 1281.

ǣglǣc, *n.a-stem*, distress 1187.

ǣglēaw, *adj.*, wise, skilled in law 805; **ǣclēawe** 321.

ǣht, *f.i-stem*, [AUGHT¹]; possessions 904, 907, 915.

æht, *f.i-stem*, counsel 473.

ǣlǣrend, *m.cons-stem*, doctor of the law 506.

ǣlc, *pron.*, each 1312.

ælfylce, *n.ja-stem*, foreign nation 36.

ælmihtig, *adj.*, almighty 145, 1145.

ǣne, *adv.*, once 1252.

ǣnig, *adj.pron.*, any 159, 166, 538, 660, 915.

ǣnlīc, *adj.*, peerless, beautiful 74, 259.

æpled, *p.pt.*, curved 1259n.

ǣr, *adv.*, before 74, 101, etc; *superl.* first 116; *conj.*, before 447, 676, etc; *prep.w.dat.*, before 1227; *comp.adj.*, former 305.

ǣrdæg, *m.a-stem*, dawn 105.

ǣrgewyrht, *fn.i-stem*, [+ IWURHT]; former deed 1301.

ǣriht, *n.a-stem*, law 375.

ǣrþan, *conj.*, until 1083.

æscrōf, *adj.*, illustrious 202, 275.

æscwiga, *m.n-stem*, warrior 259.

æt, *prep.w.dat.*, at 137; from 191; in 1177.

ætsomne, *adv.*, together 833.

ætȳwan, *w.v.(1)*, [ATEW]; reveal, appear 69; **oðȳwde** 163.

æðelcyning, *m.a-stem*, noble king 219.

æðele, *adj.*, [ATHEL]; noble 275, 300, 545, 591, 647, *1028*n, 1073, 1145; *superl.* 476, 732, 1024, 1106, 1173.

æðeling, *m.a-stem*, [ATHELING]; prince, *12*, 66, 99, 202, 845, 885.

æðelu, *n.ja-stem pl.*, [ATHEL]; race, lineage 315, 433.

ǣwita, *m.n-stem*, lawyer, counsellor 455.

B

bald, *adj.*, bold 412, 593, 1072.

baldor, *m.a-stem*, prince 344.

bān, *n.a-stem*, bone 787.

bāncofa, *m.n-stem*, [+ COVE¹]; body 1249n.

gebann, *n.a-stem*, command 557.

bannan, *v.(7)*, summon 45.

bǣl, *n.a-stem*, pyre 578.

bǣr, *f.ō-stem*, bier 872.

gebǣru, *f.ō-stem*, [IBERE]; behaviour 659, 710.

bæþ, *n.a-stem*, bath 490.

bæðweg, *m.a-stem*, watery path 244.

be, *prep.w.dat.*, concerning 168, 337, 342, etc; by 78; along 1273.

bēacen, *n.a-stem*, sign 92, 100, 162.

beadu, *f.wō-stem*, battle 34.

beadurōf, *adj.*, war-renowned 152, 1003, 1184.

beaduþrēat, *m.a-stem*, [+ THREAT]; army 31.

beaggifa, *m.n-stem*, [BEE² +]; overlord 100, 1198.

bealudǣd, *f.i-stem*, evil deed 515.

bēam, *m.a-stem*, tree, cross 91, 424, 850, 864.

bearhtm, *see* **breahtm**.

bearn, *n.a-stem*, child 179, 181, 354, 476, 525, 813.

bebēodan, *v.(2)*, [BIBEDE]; bid, command, 224, *378*, 710.

bebod, *n.a-stem*, command 1169.

bebūgan, *v.*(2), [BIBUGH]; avoid 609.

beclingan, *v.*(3), bind 696.

becuman, *v.*(4), arrive 142.

bedelfan, *v.*(3), bury 1080.

bedyrnan, *w.v.*(1), [+ DERN]; conceal 584, 602.

befæstan, *w.v.*(1), establish, secure 1212, 1300.

befēolan, *v.*(3), [BIFELE]; grant 196.

befōn, *v.*(7), [BEFONG]; grasp 842.

beforan, *adv.*, before 1141; *prep. w.dat.*, before 108.

begangan, *v.*(7), observe 1170.

bēgen, *adj.*, [BO]; both 614, 618, 804, 963, 1008.

begitan, *v.*(5), get 1151, 1247n.

begrafan, *v.*(6), bury 834, 973.

behealdan, *v.*(7), observe, guard 111, 1143.

behelian, *w.v.*(1), [BEHELE]; bury, hide 429, 830 (cp Sievers-Brunner § 400 n2).

behlīdan, *v.*(1), [+ LID sb.]; close 1229.

behȳdan, *w.v.*(1), conceal 792.

belīðan, *v.*(1), [+ LITHE[1]]; deprive of 877.

belūcan, *v.*(2), [BELOUKE]; lock up 1026.

bemīðan, *v.*(1), [+ MITHE]; conceal 583.

bēn, *f.i-stem,* petition 1088.

benūgan, *pret.-pres.*(5), have at one's disposal 618.

(ge)bēodan, *v.*(2), command, offer, announce 18, 80, 276, *971,* 1211.

beofian, *w.v.*(2), [BIVE]; quiver 758.

bēon, *anom.v.,* be 89, 339, 426, 430, 526, 542, 605, 675, 733, 808, 910, 922, 1080, 1295.

beorg, *m.a-stem,* mountain, sepulchre ? 510, 578.

beorgan, *v.*(3), [BERGH]; protect 134.

beorhhlīþ, *n.a-stem,* [+ LITH[2]]; mountain slope 787.

beorht, *adj.,* fair 88, 489, 782, 789, 821, 1254; *comp.* 1109; *superl.* 947; **beorhte,** *adv.,* clearly 92.

beorhtm, *see* **breahtm.**

beorn, *m.a-stem,* [BERNE]; man 100, 710.

beran, *v.*(4), bear, proceed 45n, 1186, 1195n.

berædan, *w.v.*(1), deprive of 498.

berēafian, *w.v.*(2), deprive of 909.

bescūfan, *v.*(2), hurl 942.

besēon, *v.*(5), look 83.

besettan, *w.v.*(1), surround *1025.*

besylcan, *w.v.*(1), exhaust 697.

betǣcan, *w.v.*(1), entrust, hand over 585.

betra, *see* **god.**

betwēonum, *prep.w.gen.,* between 1206.

beþeccan, *w.v.*(1), [BITHECCHE]; cover, overwhelm 76, 835, 1235, 1298.

beþringan, *v.*(3), [BITHRING]; encompass 949.

beweorcean, *w.v.*(1), adorn 1023.

beweotigan, *w.v.*(2), [BIWITIE]; observe 744.

bewindan, *v.*(3), surround 733.

beþurfan, *pret.pres.*(3), [+ THARF]; need 543.

bewrecan, *v.*(5), beat 251n.

(ge)bīdan, *v.*(1), wait 253, 329, 484, 864, 1092.

biddan, *v.*(5), pray, ask for 494, 789, 1089.

bigang, *mn.a-stem,* course 1123.

bill, *n.ja-stem,* sword 122, 257.

bindan, *v.*(3), bind 771.

bisceop, *m.a-stem,* bishop 1051, 1056, 1094.

bisgu, *f.ō-stem,* affliction 1244.

bisittan, *v.*(5), possess, hold 473.

bissceophād, *m.ua-stem,* bishop-ric 1211.

*bitrum, *adv.,* bitterly 1244n.

blāc, *adj.* [BLAKE]; pale, shining 91.

blanca, *m.n-stem,* [BLONK]; steed 1184.

blǣd, *m.a-stem,* [BLEAD]; life, prosperity, joy 354, 489, 825.

blēo, *n.ja-stem,* [BLEE]; form, colour 758, 1105.

blin, *n.a-stem,* cessation 825.

blind, *adj.,* blind 1214.

blindnes, *f.jō-stem,* blindness 299, 389.

blis, *f.jō-stem,* bliss 1137.

ġeblissian, *w.v.(2),* gladden 839.

blīðe, *adj.,* blithe 246, 1317; *comp.* 96.

bōc, *f.monos.-stem,* book 204, 364, 1211.

bōcstæf, *m.a-stem,* letter 91.

boda, *m.n-stem* [BODE[1]]; mes-senger 77, 262.

bodian, *w.v.(2),* proclaim 1140.

bold, *n.a-stem,* dwelling, palace 162n.

bord, *n.a-stem,* shield, ship's side, *by synecdoche,* ship? 24n, 114, 238, 1186.

bordhaga, *m.n-stem,* [+ HAW[1]]; shield defence 652.

bordhrēða, *m.n-stem,* shield covering ?, phalanx ? 122n.

bōt, *f.ō-stem,* remedy, repentance 299, 1125.

brād, *adj.,* broad 916.

breahtm, *m.a-stem,* tumult, ac-claim 39; **bearhtme** 864; **beorhtme** 205n.

ġebrec, *n.a-stem,* [+ BRACK[1]]; crash 114.

brecan, *v.(4),* break, rush 122, 244.

breġdan, *v.(3)* [BRAID]; link 257.

brēost, *mn.a-stem,* breast 595.

brēostloca, *m.n-stem,* spirit, heart 1249n.

brēostsefa, *m.n-stem,* mind, spirit 804.

brīdels, *m.a-stem,* bridle 1174.

brīdelshring, *m.a-stem,* bridle-ring 1193.

brim, *n.a-stem,* sea 253, 971, 1003.

brimþisa, *m.n-stem,* ship 238.

brimwudu, *m.u-stem,* ship 244.

bringan, *v.(3); w.v.(1),* bring 872, 1129, 1137.

broġdenmǣl, *n.a-stem,* [BROW-DEN +]; patterned sword 758.

bront, *adj.,* [BRANT]; tall 238.

brōðor, *m.r-stem,* brother 489, 510.

brūcan, *v.(2),* enjoy 1250, 1315, 1320.

brytta, *m.n-stem,* [BRIT v.]; giver, ruler 162n, 957.

bryttian, *w.v.(2),* [BRIT]; destroy 579.

burg, *f.monos-stem,* city 152, 412, 821, 863.

burgāgend, *m.cons-stem,* prince 1174.

*burgende, *m.ja-stem,* city boun-dary 31n.

burgsittend, *m.cons-stem,* citizen 276.

burgwīġend, *m.cons-stem,* war-rior 34.

būtan, *conj.,* except 661; unless 689; *prep.w.acc.,* except 539; *w.dat.,* without, except for 801, 1227.

byldan, *w.v.(1),* [BIELD]; encour-age 1038.

bȳme, *f.n-stem,* [BEME]; trumpet 109.

ġebyrde, *adj.,* [cp BIRDE]; innate 593.

byrgen, *f.jō-stem* [BURIAN]; tomb 186, 652.

byrne, *f.n-stem,* byrnie 257.

byrnwīggend, *m.cons-stem*, warrior 224; **byrnwīgendum,** 235.

C

cāf, *adj.*, [COF]; swift 56.

campwudu, *m.u-stem*, shield 51.

carcern, *n.a-stem*, prison 715.

cāserdōm, *m.a-stem*, empire 8.

cāsere, *m.ja-stem*, emperor 42, 70, 262.

cearwelm, *m.i-stem*, [+ WALM¹]; surge of grief 1257.

cēas, *f.ō-stem*, conflict 56.

ceaster, *f.ō-stem*, city 274, 384, 972.

ceasterware, *m.i-stem pl.*, citizens 42.

cennan, *w.v.* (*1*), give birth to 336, 354, 508; name 587.

cēol, *m.a-stem*, ship 250.

gecēosan, *v.* (*2*), choose 607, 1038, 1058.

ceruphīn, cherubim 749.

cild, *n.os.a-stem*, child 336.

cildhād, *m.ua-stem*, childhood 914.

cining, *m.a-stem*, king 988; **cyning** 5, 13, 453, 672.

cirice, *f.n-stem*, church 1007.

cirran, *w.v.* (*1*), [CHARE]; turn 914; **cyrrest** 666.

clǣne, *adj.*, pure 96, 749.

geclǣnsian, *w.v.* (*2*), [YCLENSE]; cleanse 678, 1034.

cleopigan, *w.v.* (*2*), call out, call upon 696, 1099, 1319.

clom, *m.a-stem*, [CLAM¹]; fetter 696.

clynnan, *w.v.* (*1*), resound 51.

gecnāwan, *v.* (*7*), recognize, perceive 708, 807, 1139.

cnēomǣg, *m.a-stem*, [+ MAY²]; kinsman 587.

cnēow, *n.wa-stem*, knee 847, 1135.

cniht, *m.a-stem*, boy 339.

cnihtgeong, *adj.*, young 640.

cnyssan, *w.v.* (*1*), toss 1257.

cōlian, *w.v.* (*2*), grow cold 882.

collenferhþ, *adj.*, proud 247.

corðor, *n.a-stem*, company 70, 274.

gecost, *adj.*, [cp CUST¹]; tried, excellent 257, 269, 1185.

cræft, *m.a-stem*, skill, power, knowledge 154, 558, 1017.

cræftig, *adj.*, skilled 314, 315, 419.

crīsten, *adj.*, Christian 979, 988, 1210.

cuman, *v.* (*4*), come, 150, 274, 279, 549, 1122, 1303.

cunnan, *pret.-pres.* (*3*), know, be able 167, 317, 374, 393, 399, 531, 535, 635, 856, 1162.

cūþ, *adj.*, known 42, 1191.

cwacian, *w.v.* (*2*), vibrate 757.

cwalu, *f.ō-stem*, [QUALE¹]; death 499.

***cwānig,** *adj.*, sorrowful 377.

cwealm, *mn.a-stem*, death 676.

gecwēme, *adj.*, [IQUEME]; pleasing 1049.

cwēn, *f.i-stem*, queen, woman 247, 275, 324, 610.

(ge)cweðan, *v.* (*5*), [QUETHE]; speak 169, 338, 667, 748, 938.

cwic, *adj.*, alive 691.

cwylman, *w.v.* (*1*), [QUELM]; kill 688.

cyme, *m.i-stem*, arrival 41, 1085, 1227.

cyn, *n.ja-stem*, kin 188, 209, *836*, 897.

gecynd, *fn.i-stem*, [ICUNDE]; nature 734.

cynestōl, *m.a-stem*, throne 330.

cyning, *see* **cining.**

cyninggenīðla, *m.n-stem*, royal foe 610n.

cyrran, *see* **cirran.**

gecyrran, *w.v.* (*1*), [ICHERRE]; change 1060.

(ge)cȳðan, *w.v.(1)*, [KITHE]; reveal 161, 409n, 446, 533, 588, 595, 607, 690, 702, 815, 558, 826, 1090.

D

gedafenlīc, *adj.*, fitting 1167.

dareðlācende, *pres.part.*, warrior 651; **dearoðlācende** 37.

daroð, *m.a-stem*, javelin *1*40n.

dǣd, *f.i-stem*, deed 386, 1283.

dǣdhwæt, *adj.*, bold 292.

dæg, *m.a-stem*, day 140, 185, 193n, 312, 358, 485.

dægweorc, *n.a-stem*, day's work 146

dægweorðung, *f.ō-stem*, [+ WORTHING[1]]; festival 1233.

dǣl, *m.i-stem*, part 1298, 1306.

dǣlan, *w.v.(1)*, divide 1286.

dēad, *adj.*, dead 651, 881.

dearoðlācende, *see* **dareðlācende**.

dēaþ, *m.a-stem*, death 187, 477, 584, 606.

dēaðcwalu, *f.ō-stem*, [+QUALE[1]]; agony 765.

dēgol, *n.a-stem*, secret 339.

delfan, *v.(3)*, delve 828.

dēma, *m.n-stem*, judge 745.

dēman, *w.v.(1)*, judge 303, 500.

dēofol, *mn.a-stem*, devil 181, 900, 1118.

dēofulgild, *n.a-stem*, idolatry 1040.

dēogol, *see* **dȳgol**.

dēop, *adj.*, deep 584, 1189, 1314; **dēope**, *adv.*, deeply, profoundly 1080.

dēophycggende, 352, **dēophycgende**, 881, *adj.*, wise.

dēoplīce, *adv.*, profoundly, *superl.* 280.

dēore, *see* **dȳre**.

dēorlīce, *adv.*, worthily, *superl.* 1158.

dierne, *see* **dyrne**.

disig, *adj.*, foolish 477.

dōgor(ge)rīm, *mn.a-stem*, lifetime 705, 779.

dōm, *m.a-stem*, judgement, Last Judgement, fame 365, 450, 725, 1314.

dōmgeorn, *adj.*, eager for glory 1291.

dōmweorðung, *f.ō-stem*, honour 146.

(ge)dōn, *anom.v.*, do, put 541, 1158, 1174; send 783.

draca, *m.n-stem*, dragon 765n.

drēam, *m.a-stem*, joy 1231.

drenc, *m.i-stem*, [DRENCH]; drowning 136.

drēogan *v.(2)*, [DREE]; endure 211, 765, 1260.

drīfan, *v.(1)*, drive 358.

drūsian, *w.v.(2)*, [DROWSE]; sink, become low 1257.

drȳge, *adj.*, dry 693.

gedryht, *f.i-stem*, [DRIGHT[1]]; host 27, 736.

dryhten, *m.a-stem*, [DRIGHTIN]; lord 81, 193, 198, 346, 725.

dryhtlēoþ, *n.a-stem*, [+ LEOTH]; heroic strain 342.

dryhtscipe, *m.i-stem*, authority 451.

dūfan, *v.(2)*, pierce 122.

duguþ, *f.iō-stem*, [DOUTH]; retinue, prosperity 450, 693, 1291; **dugoðum** 1159.

dūn, *f.ō-stem*, hill 717.

duru, *f.u-stem*, door 1229.

gedwola, *m.n-stem*, [+ DWALE[1]]; error, heresy 371; **gedweolan** 311n.

dȳgol, *adj.*, [DIGHEL]; secret 541; **dēogol** 1092.

dynian, *w.v.(1)*, resound 50.

dȳre, *adj.*, precious 292, *superl.* **dēorestan** 1233.

dyrnan, *w.v.(1)*, [DERN]; conceal 626, 970.

dyrne, *adj.*, hidden 722, 1092; **dierne** 1080.

dysig, *n.a-stem*, folly 707.

dyslīc, *adj.*, foolish 386.

E

ēac, *adv.*, also 3.

geēācnian, *w.v.*(2), [cp ECHE]; get with child 341.

ēādhrēðig, *adj.*, blessed 266.

ēādig, *adj.*, [EADI]; blessed 619, 805, 1290.

ēādwela, *m.n-stem*, wealth 1316.

eafera, eafora, *m.n-stem*, child 353, 439.

ēāge, *n.n-stem*, eye 298.

eald, *adj.*, old 207, 455, 904; **ald** 252, 1265; *comp.* 159; *yldra*, father 462; *yldra fæder*, ancestor, grandfather 436.

ealdfēond, *m.cons-stem*, ancient foe 493.

ealdgewin, *n.a-stem*, ancient conflict 647.

eal(l), *adj.*, all 26, 187, 385, 422, 483, 486, 649, 728, 730, 752, 855, 1087, 1117, 1130, 1196, 1219; **al(l)ra** 645, 815; **eallre** 446; **eallra** 370; *adv.*, wholly 1311.

earc, *f.ō-stem*, ark 399.

eard, *m.au-stem*, [ERD]; dwelling 599.

eare, *see* **geare**.

earfeþe, *n.ja-stem*, [ARVETH *a.*]; distress, torture 700.

earhfaru, *f.ō-stem*, arrow flight, attack 44, 116.

earhgeblond, *n.a-stem*, sea 239.

earm, *m.a-stem*, arm 1235.

earn, *m.a-stem*, [ERNE]; eagle 29.

geearnian, *w.v.*(2), deserve 526.

ēāstweg, *m.a-stem*, road to the east 255.

eatol, *adj.*, [ATEL]; terrible 901.

ēāðe, *adv.*, [EATH]; easily 1292.

ēāðmēdu, *f.ō-stem*, [EDMEDE]; humility 1087.

eaxlgestealla, *m.n-stem*, companion 64.

ebrisc, *adj.*, Hebrew 724; **ebreisce** 397; **ebresce** 559.

ēce, *adj.*, [ECHE]; eternal 526, 745, 799, 801; *adv.*, eternally 1217.

ednīowunga, *adv.*, afresh 300.

ēdre, *adv.*, forthwith 649.

(ge)efnan, *w.v.*(1), perform 713, 1014.

eft, *adv.*, again, afterwards 143, 1154

egesa, *m.n-stem*, [cp EISFUL *a.*]; terror 82; **eg(e)san** 57n, 321, 1128.

ēgstrēam, *m.a-stem*, river, sea 66, 241.

ēhtan, *w.v.*(1), pursue, persecute 139, 927.

elde, *see* **ilde**.

ēleð, *m.a-stem*, fire *1294*n.

ellen, *mn.-a-stem*, strength, courage 724n.

elþēod, *f.ō-stem*, [+ THEDE]; foreign nation 139.

elþēodig, *adj.*, foreign 57, 907.

ende, *m.ja-stem*, end, edge 59, 590.

endelīf, *n.a-stem*, death 585.

enge, *adj.*, narrow, cruel 712, 920, 1261n.

engel, *m.a-stem*, angel 79, 622.

engelcyn, *n.ja-stem*, order of angels 732.

eoforcumbul, *n.a-stem*, [EVER +]; boar image, helmet, 259; **eofurcumble** 76.

eofot, *n.a-stem*, sin 423.

eofulsæc, *n.a-stem*, blasphemy 524.

eorcnanstān, *m.a-stem*, jewel 1024.

ēoredcest, *f.i-stem*, army, legion 36.

eorl, *m.a-stem*, warrior, man 12, 66, 225, 256.

eorlmægen, *n.a-stem*, host of men 980.

eorne, *see* **georne**.

eorre, *see* **yrre**.

eorðcyning, *m.a-stem*, earthly king 1173.

eorðe, *f.n-stem*, earth 591, 727, 752.

eorðweg, *m.a-stem*, earthly way 735, 1014.

ēōwer, *adj.*, your 305, 315, 375, 579.

ermðu, *see* **yrmðu**.

ēst, *f.i-stem*, [ESTE]; grace 985.

ēðe, *adj.*, [EATH]; pleasant, *superl.* 1294.

ēðel, *m.a-stem*, native land 1219.

ēðgesȳne, *adj.*, clearly visible 256.

eðigean, *w.v.(2)*, [ETHE¹]; exhale, rise up 1106n.

F

fācensēaru, *n.wa-stem* [FAKEN]; treachery 721n.

fāh, *adj.*, [FOE]; guilty 768.

fāmig, *adj.*, foamy 237.

(ge)faran, *v.(6)*, go, die 21, 27, 733, 871, 1273.

fæc, *n.a-stem*, [FEC]; space of time 272, 959.

fæcne, *adj.*, deceitful, old ? 577, 1236n.

fǣder, *m.r-stem*, father 343, 388, 398, 438n, 783, 890.

fæderlīc, *adj.*, paternal 431.

fǣge, *adj.*, doomed 117.

fæger, *adj.*, fair 98, 742, 890, 910, 948; *comp.* 242.

fægere, *adv.*, fairly, well 1212.

fǣle, *adj.*, [FELE²]; true 88.

(ge)fǣr, *n.a-stem*, expedition 68, 93.

fæst, *adj.*, firm, fast 252, 722, 770, 882, 908; *adv.*, **fæste**, fast, firmly 570.

fæsten, *n.ja-stem*, strong-hold, place of safety 134n.

fæstlīce, *adv.*, firmly 427; *comp.* 796.

gefæstnian, *w.v.(2)*, fasten 1067.

fæt, *n.a-stem*, vessel 1025.

fæðm, *m.a-stem*, bosom, embrace 728, 765n.

fæðmian, *w.v.(2)*, encircle 971.

fēa, *adj.*, few 174, 817.

gefēa, *m.n-stem*, joy 195, 869.

feala, *adv.*, [FELE]; many 362, 636.

feallan, *v.(7)*, fall 127, 651.

fearoðhengest, *m.a-stem*, ship 226.

feng, *m.i-stem*, embrace 1287.

fēogan, *w.v.(3)*, hate 356, 360.

feohgestrēon, *n.a-stem*, [FEE¹ + ISTREON]; treasure 910.

gefeoht, *n.a-stem*, [IFIHT]; battle 646, 1183.

gefēon, *v.(5)*, rejoice 110, 174, 1115.

fēond, *m.cons-stem*, enemy 68, 93, 207.

fēondscipe, *m.i-stem*, enmity 356.

feor, *adv.*, distant 830; long ago; *comp.* 646.

feorh, *mn.ua-stem*, life, spirit 134, 680; **on wīdan fēore**, for ever 1288; **tō wīdan fēore**, for ever 211.

feorhlegu, *f.ō-stem*, death 458.

feorhneru, *f.ō-stem*, salvation 897.

feorran, *adv.*, [FERREN]; from afar 992.

fēower, *num.adj.*, four 743.

(ge)fēran, *w.v.(1)*, [FERE¹]; go, travel 215, 735.

ferhþ, *see* **fyrhþ**.

ferhðglēaw, *adj.*, wise 327, 880.

ferhðsefa, *see* **firhðsefa**.

(ge)ferian, *w.v.(1)*, [FERRY]; carry 108, 992.

gefeti(ge)an, *w.v.(2)*, fetch 1052, 1160.

fēða, *m.n-stem*, battle-formation 35n.

fēðegest, *m.i-stem*, stranger 844.

gefic, *n.a-stem*, deceit 577.

fīfelwǣg, *m.i-stem*, sea 237.

fīfhund, *num.*, five hundred 379.

findan, *v.(3)*, find 84, 202, 327, 373, 632, 830, 924, 973, 1031, 1079, 1254.

finger, *m.a-stem*, finger 120.

fīras, *m.ja-stem pl.*, men 897.

firen, *f.ō-stem*, sin 908, 1314.

firhðsefa, *m.n-stem*, mind 213; **fyrhðsefan** 98, 534; **ferhðsefan** 316.

fiðre, *n.ja-stem*, wing 742.

flān, *m.a-f.ō-stem*, [FLANE]; arrow 117.

fleōgan, *v.(2)*, fly 140.

fleōn, *v.(2)*, flee 127.

fliht, *m.i-stem*, flight 743.

geflit, *n.a-stem*, strife 443.

flōd, *mn.ua-stem*, water 1269.

flot, *n.a-stem*, [FLOAT]; sea 226.

fodder, *n.a-stem*, fodder 360.

folc, *n.a-stem*, folk 27, 117, 157, 362, 415, 1142.

folcscearu, *f.ō-stem*, nation 967; **folcscere** 402.

foldbūend, *m.cons-stem*, dweller on earth 1013.

folde, *f.n-stem*, [FOLD[1]]; earth 721.

foldgræf, *n.a-stem*, grave 844.

foldweg, *m.a-stem*, road 215.

folgaþ, *m.a-stem*, retinue 903.

folgian, *w.v.(2)*, follow 929.

folm, *f.ō-stem*, hand 1065, 1075.

for, *prep.w.acc.*, before 546; *w.dat.*, in front of 110; on account of 496; **for worulde**, in the world 4; **for eorðan**, on earth 591.

foran, *adv.*, [FORNE]; in front 1183.

fore, *prep.w.dat.*, before 577; **fore**, *adv.*, before 345n.

foreþanc, *m.a-stem*, deliberation 356.

forgifan, *v.(5)*, give 144, 354.

forlǣran, *w.v.(1)*, seduce 208.

forlǣtan, *v.(7)*, leave, allow 432n, 598, 689, 700, 712, 792, 928.

forniman, *v.(4)*, [FORNIM]; destroy, consume 131, 578n.

forsēcan, *w.v.(1)*, afflict 932.

forsēon, *v.(5)*, despise 389, 1318.

fortyhtan, *w.v.(1)*, [FORTIHT]; lead astray 208.

forþ, *adv.*, forth, thenceforth 120, 192.

forþan, *adv.*, therefore 309.

forþryccan, *w.v.(1)*,[+THRUTCH]; oppress 1276.

forðsnotter, *adj.*, very wise 379; **forðsnoterne** 1052.

forþylman, *w.v.(1)*, envelop 766.

forwyrd, *f.i-stem*, perdition 764.

fōt, *m.monos-stem*, foot 1065.

fōtmæl, *n.a-stem*, foot 830.

fram, *prep.w.dat.*, from 140; **from** 590; by means of 190.

frætwan, *w.v.(1)*, adorn 1198.

frætwe, *f.ō-stem pl.*, adornment 88, 1270.

gefrætwian, *w.v.(2)*, adorn 742.

frēa, *m.n-stem*, lord 488, 680, 1307.

frēcne, *adj.*, terrible 93.

(ge)fremman, *w.v.(1)*, [FREME]; do, achieve, express an emotion 299, 363, 386, 402, 415, 472, 515, 524, 569.

gefrēge, *adj.*, renowned 967.

frēobearn, *n.a-stem*, child of noble birth 672.

frēond, *m.cons-stem*, friend 360, 953.

frēondlēas, *adj.*, friendless 924.

frēondrǣdden, *f.jō-stem*, friendship 1207.

freoðian, *w.v.*(2), [FRITH¹]; protect 1146.

fricca, *m.n-stem*, herald 54.

(ge)fricg(g)an, *v.*(5), ask, learn 155, 157, 560, 990.

frīge, *f.ō-stem pl.*, love 341.

(ge)frignan, *v.*(3), [FRAYNE]; ask, learn 172, 443, 534, 542, 589, 1013.

friþ, *m.u-n.a-stem*, protection 1183.

friðeleās, *adj.*, savage 127.

friðowebba, *m.n-stem*, angel 88.

frōd, *adj.*, wise 343, 431, 443, 542, 637, 1163.

frōfor, *f.ō-stem*, [FROVER]; comfort 196, 502, 1036.

from, *adj.*, bold 261.

from, *prep.*, see **fram**.

fromlīce, *adv.*, boldly 454.

fruma, *m.n-stem*, [FRUME]; beginning 1141; prince 210; author 771, 792, 838.

frymþ, *f.ō-stem*, [FRUMTH]; beginning, creation 502; **frumþa** 345.

ful, *adj.*, full 751, 938; *adv.*, fully 167.

fūl, *n.a-stem*, foulness, guilt 768n.

gefullæstan, *w.v.*(1), [FILST]; help 1150.

fultum, *m.a-stem*, help 1052.

gefulwian, *w.v.*(2), [FULL¹]; baptize 1043.

fulwiht, *mn.a-f.i-stem*, [FULLOUGHT]; baptism 172, 490.

furðum, *adv.*, [FORTHEN]; just; **syððan furþum**, as soon as 913.

furður, *adv.*, further, more 388.

fūs, *adj.*, [FOUS]; ready 1218, 1236.

(ge)fylgan, *w.v.*(1), follow, persist in 371, 576.

fyllan, *w.v.*(1), lay low 1040.

gefyllan, *w.v.*(1), fill, fulfil 680, 1070, 1083, 1142.

fȳr, *n.a-stem*, fire 1105, 1311.

fȳrbæþ, *n.a-stem*, fire-bath 948.

fyrd, *f.i-stem*, [FERD¹]; army 35.

fyrdhwæt, *adj.*, brave 21.

fyrdlēoþ, *n.a-stem*, battle song 27.

fyrdrinc, *m.a-stem*, [+ RINK¹]; warrior 261.

fȳrhāt, *adj.*, fire-hot 936.

fyrhþ, *mn.a-stem*, mind, spirit 196; **ferhð** 174, 427; **wīdan fyrhð**, for ever 760; **wīdan ferhð** 800.

fyrhðsefa, see **firhðsefa**.

fyrhðwērig, *adj.*, sad, wretched 560.

fyrmest, *adv.*, first, especially 68, 316.

fyrn, *adv.*, [FERN]; long since 632.

fyrndagas, *m.a-stem pl.*, former days 398.

fyrngeflit, *n.a-stem*, ancient strife 903.

fyrngemynd, *f.i-n.ja-stem*, memory of former times 327.

fyrngewrit, *n.a-stem*, ancient record 155, 431.

fyrngid, *n.ja-stem*, ancient lore 542.

fyrnwita, *m.n-stem*, prophet, sage 1153; **fyrnweota** 343; **fyrnwiota** 438.

fyrst, *m.ia-stem*, [FRIST]; period of time 67, 490.

fyrstmearc, *f.ō-stem*, appointed interval 1033.

fyrwet, *n.ja-stem*, anxiety 1078.

(ge)fȳsan, *w.v.*(1), [FUSE¹]; hasten, make eager, drive on 226, 260, 1269.

G

gād, *n.wa-stem*, lack 991.

galan, *v.*(6), chant, cry 52, 124n.

galdor, *n.a-stem*, [GALDER]; speech 161.

galga, *m.n-stem*, gallows, cross 179.

gamel, *adj.*, old 1246.

gān, *anom.v.,* go 320, 1095.

gang, *m.a-stem,* course 633, 1255; **gongum,** 648.

gangan, *v.(7),* go 313.

gār, *m.a-stem,* [GARE¹]; spear 23, 118.

gārþracu, *f.ō-stem,* battle 1185.

gārþrīst, *adj.,* [+ THRISTE]; bold 204.

gāst, *m.a-stem,* spirit 176, 182, 199, 302, 352, 471, 935.

gāstgerȳne, *n.ja-stem,* spiritual mystery 189.

gāsthālig, *adj.,* holy in spirit 562.

gāstlēas, *adj.,* dead 874.

gāstsunu, *m.u-stem,* spiritual son 673.

gǣlan, *w.v.(1),* [GELE]; hesitate 692.

ge...ge, *conj.,* both...and 964-5,

gē, *pron.,* ye 290, 293, 295, 298, 309, *318.*

geador, *adv.,* together 26.

geagncwide, *see* **gēncwide.**

geagninga, *adv.,* completely 673.

gēar, *n.a-stem,* year 1, 7, 1264.

gēara, *adv.,* [YORE]; formerly 1265.

gēardagas, *m.a.stem pl.,* former days 290, 1266.

geare, 167, **eare,** 399, **gere,** 859, **gearwe,** 1239, *adv.,* [YARE]; clearly, completely, exactly; *comp.* 945; *superl.* 328.

gearolīce, *adv.,* completely 288.

gearu, *adj.,* [YARE]; ready 23, 85 222, 605.

gearusnottor, *adj.,* very wise 586; **gearosnotor** 418.

gearwe, *see* **geare.**

(ge)gearwian, *w.v.(2),* [YARE]; prepare, provide 47, 888, 999.

gēasne, *adj.,* [GEASON]; lacking 923.

geatolic, *adj.,* magnificent 258, 331.

gehðu, *f.ō-stem,* [cp GETHE]; sorrow, anxiety 609, 667; **gehdum** 531n.

gēn, *adv.,* again, still 373, 1077.

gēncwide, *m.i-stem,* [+ QUIDE]; answer 594; **geagncwide** 525.

gēōc, *f.ō-stem,* help 1138.

gēōcend, *m.cons-stem,* helper 682.

geofen, *n.a-stem,* ocean 227.

geogoþ, *f.ō-stem,* youth 638, 1264.

geogoðhād, *m.ua-stem,* youth 1266.

geolorand, *m.a-stem,* shield *yellow because made of linden wood or decorated with gold* 118.

gēōmor, *adj.,* [YOMER]; sorrowful 182, 322, 627, 921.

gēōmormōd, *adj.,* sorrowful 413.

geond, *prep.w.acc.,* [YOND]; throughout 16; through 733.

georn, *adj.,* [YERN]; eager 268.

georne, 199, **eorne,** 322, *adv.,* eagerly.

geornlīce, *adv.,* eagerly 1096.

gēōtan, *v.(2),* [YET, YOTE]; pour out 1132.

gere, *see* **geare.**

gidd, *n.ja-stem,* [YED]; song, traditional knowledge 418, 586.

gif, *conj.,* if 435, 441, 459.

gifan, *v.(5),* give 360n, 365.

gifu, *f.ō-stem,* gift, grace 176, 265, 1143.

gildan, *v.(3),* repay 493.

gim, *m.a-stem,* gem 90.

gīman, *w.v.(1),* [YEME]; heed 616.

gimcynn, *n.ja-stem,* precious stone 1023.

gīna, *adv.,* again; þa **gīna,** yet again 1069.

ging, *adj.,* young 353, 464; *comp.* 159.

gīō, *adv.,* formerly 436.

girwan, *w.v.(1),* build 1021.

gīsel, *m.a-stem,* [YISEL]; hostage 600.

glæd, *adj.*, glad; *comp.* 955.

glædmōd, *adj.*, joyful 1095.

glǣm, *m.i-stem*, radiance 1266.

glēaw, *adj.*, [GLEW]; wise 594, 638, 806, 1162; *superl.* 536.

glēawhȳdig, *adj.*, wise 934.

glēawlīce, *adv.*, wisely 189.

glēawnes, *f.jō-stem*, wisdom 961.

glēd, *f.i-stem*, [GLEED]; fire-coal 1302.

geglengan, *w.v.(1)*, adorn 90.

gnornian, *w.v.(2)*, grieve 1259.

gnornsorg, *f.ō-stem*, grief 655, 976.

gnyrn, *f.i-stem*, grief, sin *422*, 1138.

gnyrnwrǣc, *f.jō-stem*, [+ WRECHE]; vengeance for grief 359.

god, *m.a-stem*, God 4, 109, 209, 961.

gōd, *adj.*, good 637; *comp.* **betera** 506, 618, 1038; *superl.* **sēlest**, **sēlost**, **sēlust**, 527, 1018, 1027, 1164, *1169*, 1201.

gōd, *n.a-stem*, goods, property 923.

godbearn, *n.a-stem*, divine son 719.

godcund, *adj.*, divine 1032.

gōddend, *m.cons-stem*, benefactor 359.

godgim, *m.a-stem*, divine jewel, sun, heavenly body 1113n.

godspel, *n.a-stem*, gospel 176.

gold, *n.a-stem*, gold 90, 1259, 1309.

goldhoma, *m.n-stem*, [+HAME[1]]; garment ornamented with gold 991.

goldhord, *m.a-stem*, treasure 790.

goldwine, *m.i-stem*, overlord 201.

gomen, *n.a-stem*, joy 1264.

gong, *see* **gang**.

gram, *adj.*, [GRAME]; fierce 43, 118.

grāp, *f.ō-stem*, [GROPE[1]]; grip 759.

grēot, *n.a-stem*, earth 834.

grim, *adj.*, grim 525.

grīma, *m.n-stem*, helmet 125.

grīmhelm, *m.a-stem*, visored helmet 258.

gring, *mn.a-stem*, slaughter 115.

gringan, *v.(3)*, fall 126.

gripe, *m.i-stem*, grip 1302.

grund, *m.ua-stem*, ground, abyss, world 943, 1113, 1289.

gryrefæst, *adj.*, [GRURE +]; terrible 759.

guma, *m.n-stem*, [GOME[1]]; man 14, 464, 531, 562.

gumrīce, *n.ja-stem*, [+ RICHE]; earthly kingdom 1220.

gūþ, *f.ō-stem*, battle 23.

gūðcwēn, *f.i-stem*, warlike queen 254.

gūðgelǣca, *m.n-stem*, warrior 43.

gūðheard, *adj.*, brave in battle 204.

gūðrōf, *adj.*, courageous 273.

gūðscrūd, *n.monos-stem*, coat-of-mail 258.

gūðweard, *m.a-stem*, prince 14.

gylden, *adj.*, golden 125.

gylt, *m.i-stem*, guilt 816.

H

habban, *w.v.(3)*, have 49, 63, 288, 316, 369, 408, 415, 594, 621, 807, 824, 1252.

hād, *m.ua-stem*, form, manner, order of being 72, 336, 739n, 1245n.

hādor, *n.a-stem*, brightness 629n.

half, *see* **healf**.

hālig, *adj.*, holy 86, 107, 218, 333, 364, 429, 457, 625, *720*, 739, 750, 757, 820, 842, 975, 987, 1005, 1011, 1031, 1093, 1194.

hām, *m.a-stem*, home 143, 920.

hand, *f.u-stem*, hand 457, 804.

handgeswing, *n.a-stem,* combat 115.

hāt, *n.a-stem,* heat 628.

hāt, *adj.,* hot 1132, 1297; *superl.* 579.

hātan, *v.*(7), [HIGHT¹]; command, call, name 42, 214, 505, 755, 1172.

hǣdor, *adj.,* clear 747.

hæft, *m.a-stem,* captivity 703.

gehæftan, *w.v.*(1), [cp HAFT²]; oppress 613.

hæftnēd, *f.i-stem,* imprisonment 297.

hǣl, *n.i-stem,* [HEAL]; greeting 1002.

hǣlend, *m.cons-stem,* [HEALEND]; saviour 725, 808, 1062.

hǣleþ, *m.cons-stem,* [HELETH]; warrior, man 73, 273, 511, 538, 640, 661, 671.

hǣlo, *f.ō-stem,* health 1215.

hǣs, *f.i-stem,* [HEST]; command 86.

hǣðen, *adj.,* heathen 126, 1075.

hē, hēo, hit, *pron.,* he, she, it 9, 14, 18, 147, 170, 271, 350, 440 (reflexive), 677 895; **hēo** 570; **hīo** 268; **hire** 1199; **hiere** 222; *pl.* 48, 173, 360, 998; **he** 59n; **hīo** 384; **hēo** 254; **hiera** 360; **hira** 174.

hēafodwylm, *m.i-stem,* tears 1132.

hēah, *adj.,* high 424; *superl.* 197n.

hēahengel, *m.a-stem,* archangel 750.

hēahmægen, *n.a-stem,* sublime power 464, 752.

(ge)healdan, *v.*(7), hold, observe guard 156, 192, 449, 823, 1168.

healf, *f.ō-stem,* side 548, 1179; **halfa** 954.

healfcwic, *adj.,* half dead 133.

healsian, *w.v.*(2), [HALSE¹]; beseech 699.

healt, *adj.,* halt 1214.

hēan, *adj.,* [HEAN]; wretched 701, 1215.

hēannes, *f.jō-stem,* height 1124.

hēap, *m.a-stem,* band, throng, 141, 269, 1205.

heard, *adj.,* cruel 83, 115, 180, 557, 704, 808; *comp.* 565; **hearde,** *adv.,* severely 400.

heardecg, *f.jō-stem,* sword 757.

hearding, *m.a-stem,* warrior 25.

hearm, *m.a-stem,* grief 911.

hearmloca, *m.n-stem,* prison 695.

heaðofremmende, *pres.part.,* fighting 130.

geheaðrian, *w.v.*(2), confine 1275.

heaðuwylm, *m.i-stem,* fierce flame 1305; **heaðowelma** 579.

hebban, *v.*(6), raise 25, 107, 123.

hel, *f.jō-stem,* hell 900.

helan, *v.*(4), [HELE¹]; conceal 703.

helm, *m.a-stem,* covering, defender 148, 230n.

help, *f.ō-stem,* help 679, 1031.

hēo, *n.ja-stem,* form 6.

heofon, *m.a-stem,* heaven 699, 727, 1229; **heofun** 752; **heofenum** 83.

heofoncining, *m.a-stem,* 747; king of heaven; **heofoncyninges** 170; **heofoncyninge** 367.

heofonlīc, *adj.,* heavenly 739, 1144.

heofonrīce, *n.ja-stem,* [HEAVEN-RIC]; heavenly kingdom 197, 621.

heofonsteorra, *m.n-stem,* heavenly body 1112.

heolster, *mn.a-stem,* [HOLSTER]; darkness, concealment 1081.

heolstorhof, *n.a-stem,* hell 763n.

heorte, *f.n-stem,* heart 628, 1223.

heorucumbul, *n.a-stem,* standard 107.

heorudrēorig, *adj.,* wounded *or* very sorrowful 1214.

heorugrim, *adj.*, very fierce *119*.

hēr, *adv.*, here 661.

here, *m.ja-stem*, [HERE]; army 32, 52, 58, 65, 101, 115, 143, 148, 205, 406.

herecombol, *n.a-stem*, battle standard 25.

herefeld, *m.ua-stem*, battlefield *126*, 269.

heremægen, *n.a-stem*, multitude 170.

heremeðel, *n.a-stem*, assembly 550.

hererǣswa, *m.n-stem*, leader 994.

heresīþ, *m.a-stem*, campaign 133.

heretēma, *m.n-stem*, leader 10.

hereþrēat, *m.a-stem*, army 265.

hereweorc, *n.a-stem*, warfare 656.

herian, *w.v.(1)*, [HERY]; praise 453, 892, 1096, 1220; **herigean** 919.

herwan, *see* **(ge)hyrwan**.

hete, *m.i-stem*, [HATE[1]]; hatred 424.

hetend, *m.cons-stem*, enemy 18, 119.

hīehðo, *f.ō-stem*, height 1086.

gehigd, *fn.i-stem*, thought 1223.

hige, 808, 840, **hyge**, 685, *m.i-stem*, [HIGH[1]]; mind, thought.

higefrōfor, *f.ō-stem*, consolation 355.

higegeōmor, 1297, **hygegēomre** 1215, *adj.*, sad.

higeglēaw, *adj.*, wise 333.

higeþanc, *m.a-stem*, thought 156.

hild, *f.jō-stem*, battle 18, 32.

hildedēor, *adj.*, bold in battle 935.

hildegesa, *m.n-stem*, terror in battle 113.

hildenǣdre, *f.n-stem*, battle serpent, arrow 119, 141.

hilderinc, *m.a-stem*, warrior 263.

hildeserce, *f.n-stem*, coat-of-mail 234.

hildfruma, *m.n-stem*, prince, leader 10.

hīwbeorht, *adj.*, radiant 73.

gehladan, *v.(6)*, [LADE]; load 234.

hlāf, *m.a-stem*, loaf 613, 616.

hlāford, *m.a-stem*, lord 265, 475.

hlǣfdige, *f.n-stem*, lady 400.

hleahtor, *m.a-stem*, exultation 919.

hlēapan, *v.(7)*, run 54.

hlēo, *mn.wa-stem*, [LEE[1]]; refuge, protection 99, 507, 616, 1073.

hlēor, *n.a-stem*, [LEER[1]]; face 1098.

hlēoðrian, *w.v.(2)*, cry out 900.

gehlēða, *m.n-stem*, companion 113.

hlihan, *v.(6)*, rejoice 994.

hlūd, *adj.*, loud 1272; **hlūde**, *adv.*, loudly, clearly 406.

hlȳt, *m.i-stem*, portion 820.

hnāg, *adj.*, humiliating 668.

hnesce, *adj.*, [NESH]; soft 615.

hof, *n.a-stem*, [HOVE[3]]; house 557.

holm, *m.a-stem*, sea 982.

holmþracu, *f.ō-stem*, stormy sea 727.

holt, *mn.a-stem*, forest 113.

hōn, *v.(7)*, hang 424, 851.

hord, *n.a-stem*, treasure 1091.

horh, *mn.a-stem*, [HORE]; filth; *instr.* 297.

hornbora, *m.n-stem*, trumpeter 54.

hospcwide, *m.i-stem*, [+QUIDE]; insult, blasphemy 523.

hrā, *mn.wa-stem*, body, corpse 579.

hrædlīce, *adv.*, [RADLY]; quickly 1086.

hraðe, 76, **raðe**, 372, *adv.*, [RATHE]; quickly.

hrefen, 52, **hrefn**, 110, *m.a-stem*, raven.

hrēmig, *adj.*, exultant 149, 1137.

hrēof, *adj.*, [REOF]; leprous 1214.

hrēosan, *v.(2)*, [REOSE]; fall 763.

hreðer, *m.a-stem*, breast 1144.

hreðerloca, *m.a-stem*, breast 86n.

hring, *m.a-siem*, globe 1131n.

hringedstefna, *m.n-stem*, [+ STEM]; ring-prowed ship 248.

hrōf, *m.a-stem*, roof 89.

hrōpan, *v.(7)*, [ROPE²]; call out, make a proclamation 54.

hrōr, *adj.*, [cp ROAR sb.²]; bold 65.

hrōðer, *m.a-stem*, comfort 16.

hrūse, *f.n-stem*, earth 218.

hū, *conj.adv.*, how 176, 179, 185, 335.

hund, *num.*, hundred 2.

hungor, *m.ua-stem*, hunger 613, 616.

hūru, *conj.*, [HURE]; indeed 1046.

hūs, *n.a-stem*, house 880, 1236n.

hūþ, *f.ō-stem*, plunder 149.

hwā, hwæt, *pron.*, who, what 161n, 400; *w.gen.*, what kind of 902; **to hwan**, to what purpose 1157.

gehwā, *pron.*, each 358, 569, 972, 1228.

hwǣr, *conj.*, where 205, 217, 429, 563.

gehwǣr, *adv.*, everywhere 1182.

hwæt, *adj.*, [WHAT²]; active 22.

hwæt, *interj.*, [WHAT¹]; lo 293, 334, 364, etc.

hwæteādig, *adj.*, fortunate 1194.

hwætmōd, *adj.*, bold 1005.

gehwæðer, *pron.*, each of two 628, 963.

hwæðre, *adv.*, however 719.

gehweorfan, *v.(3)*, [WHARVE]; turn 1125.

hwīl, *f.ō-stem*, space of time 479; **hwīle nū**, just now 582.

hwīt, *adj.*, white 73.

hwone, *conj.*, until 254.

hwōpan, *v.(7)*, threaten 82n.

hwylc, *pron.*, which 850, 857.

gehwylc, *pron.*, each, every 278, 319, 409, 598, 1283, 1310, 1313.

hwyrft, *m.i-stem*, course 1.

(ge)hȳdan, *w.v.(1)*, [IHEDE]; hide 218, 831, 1091, 1107.

hyder, *adv.*, hither 548.

hyge, *see* **hige**.

hygegēomor, *see* **higegēomor**.

hygerūn, *f.ō-stem*, secret of the heart 1098.

hyht, *m.i-stem*, [HIGHT³]; hope 197n, 797.

hyhtful, *adj.*, hopeful 922.

hyhtgifa, *m.n-stem*, giver of hope 851.

gehȳnan, *w.v.(1)*, [HEAN]; humble 720.

hȳnðu, *f.ō-stem* humiliation 210.

(ge)hȳran, *w.v.(1)*, hear, obey 333, 364, 442, 511, 538, 572, 709, 784, 838, 1001, 1209.

hyrde, *m.ja-stem*, shepherd 348.

hyrst, *f.i-stem*, ornament 263.

gehyrstan, *w.v.(1)*, adorn 331.

(ge)hyrwan, *w.v.(1)*, despise 221, 355, 387.

hyse, *m.i-stem*, boy 523.

hȳþ, *f.jō-stem*, [HITHE]; harbour 248.

gehȳwan, *see* **geȳwan**.

I

ic, *pron.*, I, 163, 164, 240, 288, 347, 361, 469.

īcan, *w.v.(1)*, [ECHE]; increase 904.

ides, *f.iō-stem* lady 229, 241, 405.

geīēwan, *see* **geȳwan**.

ilca, *adj.*, same 183, 436.

ilde, *m.i-stem pl.*, men 521; **elda** 476; **yldum** 791.

in, *prep. w.acc.*, into 6; in 336; *w.dat.*, in 177, on 330; into 1296.

in, *adv.*, in 122.

inbryrdan, *see* **onbryrdan**.

ingemynd, *f.i-n.ja-stem*, remembrance 1252.

ingemynde, *adj.*, present to the mind 895.

ingeþanc, *m.a-stem*, purpose 680.

innan, *adv.*, within 1056.

innoð, *m.a-stem*, [INNETH]; heart 1145.

instæpes, *adv.*, forthwith 127.

inwit, *n.a-stem*, guile 207.

inwitþanc, *m.a-stem*, malice 308.

inwrēon, *see* **onwrēon**.

L

lā, *interj.*, lo 902.

lāc, *n.a-f.o-stem*, [LAKE¹]; gift 1136, 1199.

lācan, *v.(7)*, [LAKE¹]; fly, leap up 580, 899.

lagofæsten, 249, **lagufæsten**, 1016, *n.ja-stem*, water fastness.

lagostrēam, *m.a-stem*, river 137.

lama, *m.n-stem*, lame man 1213.

land, *n.a-stem*, land 250, 1270.

lang, *adj.*, long 432; **lange** *adv.*, long 602; *comp.* 576.

lār, *f.ō-stem*, instruction, doctrine 286, 335, 432, 497.

lārsmiþ, *m.a-stem*, scholar 203.

lāst, *m.a-stem*, track; **on laste**, behind 30.

late, *adv.*, late 708.

lāttēow, *m.wa-stem*, [LATTEW]; lord, leader 1209; **lāttīow** 520, 898.

lāþ, *adj.*, hateful 30, 94, 142; *superl.* 977.

laðian, *w.v.(2)*, [LATHE]; invite 383, 551, 556.

lāðlīc, *adj.*, hateful 520.

(ge)lǣdan, *w.v.(1)*, bring 241, 714, 968, 1183.

lǣne, *adj.*, transitory 1270.

lǣran, *w.v.(1)*, [LERE]; teach 173, 522, 529, 1205.

lǣs, **lǣst**, *see* **lȳtel**.

(ge)lǣstan, *w.v.(1)*, [LAST¹]; per-

form, achieve 368, 1165, 1196, 1207.

lǣtan, *v.(7)*, cause 237, 250, 818, 1104.

lēaf, *n.a-stem*, leaf 1226.

gelēafa, *m.n-stem*, faith 491, 965, 1035, 1136.

gelēafful, 959, **gelēaffull**, 1047, *adj.*, full of faith.

leahtor, *m.a-stem*, [LAHTER]; sin 838.

leahtorlēas, *adj.*, sinless 1208.

lēan, *n.a-stem*, [LEAN¹]; reward 824.

lēas, *adj.*, [LEASE]; lacking, false 422, 497, 1300.

lēas, *n.a-stem*, [LEASE²]; lie 576, 580.

lēasung, *f.ō-stem*, lie 689; **lēasingum** 1122.

lēf, *adj.*, infirm 1213.

lēgen, *adj.*, fiery 756.

leger, *n.a-stem*, [LAIR¹]; resting place 602.

lencten, *m.a-stem*, spring 1226.

lēod, *f.ō-stem*, [LEDE]; *pl.* people 20, 163, 181, 666.

gelēodan, *v.(2)*, grow 1226.

lēodfruma, *m.n-stem*, leader 191.

lēodgebyrga, *m.n-stem*, prince 203; **leodgebyrgean** 556.

lēodhata, *m.n-stem*, tyrant 1300.

lēodhwæt, *adj.*, courageous 11n.

lēodmǣg, *m.a-stem*, compatriot 380.

lēodmægen, *n.a-stem*, host of men 272.

lēof, *adj.*, dear 511, 1035, 1205; *comp.* 606; *superl.* 523.

lēoflīc, *adj.*, lovely 286.

lēofspell, *n.a-stem*, glad tidings 1016.

lēoht, *n.a-stem*, light 7, 298, 486, 733, 947, 1122.

lēoht, *adj.*, light, bright, clear 163, 491, 736, 1115, 1136, 1245n;

lēohte, *adv.*, brightly, gladly 92, 965.

lēoht, *adj.*, light 173.

lēoma, *m.n-stem*, [LEAM¹]; light gleam, radiance 1294.

leomu, *see* lim.

leornian, *w.v.(2)*, learn 397.

leornungcræft, *m.a-stem*, learning 380.

leoðorūn, *f.ō-stem*, wise counsel ? 522n.

leoðucræft, *m.a-stem*; art of poetry ?, skill ? 1250n.

lesan, *v.(5)*, [LEASE¹]; gather 1237.

gelettan, *w.v.(1)*, hinder, withstand 94.

līc, *n.a-stem*, [LICH]; body 877, 882.

gelīc, *adj.*, like 1320.

gelīce, *adv.*, like; *superl.* **geliccost** 1271.

līchoma, *m.n-stem*, [LICHAM]; body 736.

līf, *n.a-stem*, life 137, 305, 526, 575, 877.

līfdæg, *m.a-stem*, lifetime 441.

līffruma, *m.n-stem*, giver of life 335.

lifgan, *w.v.(3)*, live 311, 450, 486.

līfweard, *m.a-stem*, guardian of life 1035.

līfwynn, *f.i-stem*, joy in life 1268.

līg, *mn.i-stem*, [LEYE]; flame 580, 1300.

līgcwalu, *f.ō-stem*, fiery torment 296.

līge, *m.i-stem*, lie 307, 575, 666.

līgesearu, *n.wa-stem*, wile 208.

līgesynnig, *adj.*, deceitful 898.

lim, *n.a-stem*, limb 882.

gelimpan, *v.(3)*, happen 271, 441, 962, 1154.

limsēoc, *adj.*, maimed 1213.

lindgeborga, *m.n-stem*, warrior 11n.

lindwered, *n.a-stem*, troop with shields 142.

lindwīgend, *m.cons-stem*, warrior 270.

gelīðan, *v.(1)*, [LITHE¹]; depart, complete a journey 249, 1268.

līxan, *w.v.(1)*, shine 23, 1115.

loc, *n.a-stem*, clasp 1026.

loca, *m.n-stem*, [LOKE]; imprisonment 181.

lōcian, *w.v.(2)*, look 87.

lof, *mn.a-stem*, [LOF]; praise 212, 747.

lofian, *w.v.(2)*, [LOVE²]; praise 453.

lūcan, *v.(2)*, [LOUK¹]; set a jewel 264.

lufe, *f.n-stem*, love 491.

lufian, *w.v.(2)*, love 597.

lufu, *f.ō-stem*, love 936.

lungre, *adv.*, forthwith 30.

lust, *m.ua-stem*, pleasure 138, 702.

gelȳfan, *w.v.(1)*, believe 518, 795.

lyft, *mfn.i-stem*, [LIFT¹]; sky, air 733, 1270.

lyftlācende, *adj.*, moving hither and thither in the air 795.

lȳsan, *w.v.(1)*, [LEESE²]; redeem 296.

lȳt, *adv.*, [LITE⁴]; few 63.

lȳtel, *adj.*, little 272, 959; *comp.* 48; **lȳtle**, *adv.*, a little 664.

lȳthwōn, *adv.*, few 142.

M

mā, *see* **miclum**

magan, *pret.pres.(5)*, be able 33, 160, 166, 448, 511, 581, 632, 677, 978, 1158, 1177n, 1291.

man, *m.cons-stem*, man 16, 326, 660, 871; *indef.pron.*, one 358.

mān, *n.a-stem*, [MAN²]; evil 626, 1296, 1317.

mānfrēa, *m.n-stem*, wicked ruler 941.

mānfremmende, *adj.*, sinful 906.

gemang, *n.a-stem,* crowd; **on...
gemang,** among 96.

manig, *adj.pron.,* many 231, 969, 1016; **monige** 499; **manegum** 15.

manrīm, *mn.a-stem,* number of men 650.

mānþēaw, *m.wa-stem,* sinful custom 929.

mānweorc, *adj.,* sinful 811.

maþelian, *w.v.(2),* [MATHELE]; speak 332.

māðum, *m.a-stem,* treasure 1258.

mǣg, *m.a-stem,* [MAY¹]; kinswoman 330.

mægen, *n.a-stem,* strength, host 55, 347, 1222; **mægn** 408.

mægencyning, *m.a-stem,* mighty king 1247.

mægenþrym, *m.i-stem,* majesty 734.

mægn, *see* **mægen.**

mǣl, *n.a-stem,* [MEAL²]; season 986.

mǣlan, *w.v.(1),* [MELE]; speak 351, 537.

mǣre, *adj.,* [MERE¹]; famous, glorious 214, 340, 863, 969, 989, 1063, 1222; *superl.* 1012.

mǣrðu, *f.ō-stem,* glory 15.

mearcpæþ, *m.a-stem,* road through border territory 233.

mearh, *m.a-stem,* horse 55, 1175.

medoheal, *f.ō-stem,* meadhall 1258.

melda, *m.n-stem,* [cp MELD v.¹]; informer 428.

(ge)mengan, *w.v.(1),* [MENG]; mingle, compound 306, 1296.

menigo, 870, **mengo,** 377, **mengu,** 225; *f.ō-stem,* crowd, multitude.

mennisc, *adj.,* human 6.

meotod, *m.a-stem,* creator, God 366; **meotudes** 461; **metudes** 1318.

merestrǣt, *f.ō-stem,* [MERE¹ +]; sea-road 242.

metan, *v.(5),* measure 1262.

(ge)mētan, *w.v.(1),* [YMETE]; meet, find 116, 832, 870, 985.

metelēas, *adj.,* without food 612.

gemetgian, *w.v.(2),* [cp METE¹]; moderate 1293.

metud, *see* **meotod.**

mēðe, *adj.,* weary, miserable 612, 811.

meðel, *n.a-stem,* council 546.

meðelhēgende, *adj.,* deliberating 279n.

meðelstede, *m.i-stem,* meeting place 554.

miclum, 875 **myclum,** 839, *adv.,* much; *comp.* **mā,** [MO]; more 434.

mid, *prep. w.acc.,* with 275; *w.dat.,* amongst 328; at 105; *w.instr.,* by means of 92.

middangeard, *m.a-stem,* [MIDDENERD]; world 6, 809.

middel, *m.a-stem,* middle 863, 1296.

mīdl, *n.a-stem,* bit 1175.

miht, *f.i-stem,* might 15, 295, 337, 584.

mihtig, *adj.,* mighty 680, 941.

milde, *adj.,* gracious 1042.

mīlpæþ, *m.a-stem,* road with milestones ? 1262.

milts, *f.jō-stem,* [MILCE]; mercy 501.

mīn, *adj.,* my, mine 163, 349, 436, 438, 447, 535, 656, 816, 906, 917, 929.

mīðan, *v.(1),* [MITHE]; conceal 28.

mōd, *n.a-stem,* mind, heart, spirit 268, 377n, 554, 597.

mōdblind, *adj.,* spiritually blind 306.

mōdcræft, *m.a-stem,* intelligence 408.

mōdgemynd, *fn.i-stem,* mind, intelligence 381, 839.

mōdgeþanc, *m.a-stem,* opinion 535.

mōdig, *adj.,* proud 138, 1192, 1262.

mōdor, *f.r-stem,* mother 214, 340.

mōdsefa, *m.n-stem,* mind 875.

mōdsorg, *f.o-stem,* sorrow 61.

molde, *f.n-stem,* [MOULD¹]; earth 55.

moldweg, *m.a-stem,* earth 467.

mōnaþ, *m.cons-stem,* month *1228*n.

monig, *see* **manig.**

monigfeald, *adj.,* manifold 644.

morgenspel, *n.a-stem,* news brought in the morning 969.

mōrland, *n.a-stem,* wilderness 612.

morðor, *mn.a-stem,* sin, crime 428.

morðorhof, *n.a-stem,* place of torment 1303.

morðorsleht, *m.i-stem,* [SLEIGHT²]; slaughter 650.

gemōt, *n.a-stem,* meeting 279.

mōtan, *pret.pres.(6),* be possible 175, 433, 905, 915, 1004.

mund, *f.ō-stem,* hand 729.

mūþ, *m.a-stem,* mouth 660.

mycel, *adj.,* much, large 44, 426, 597, 646n, 734; *superl.* 31, 35, 274, 381, 983.

gemyltan, *w.v.(1),* melt 1312.

gemynd, *fn.i-stem,* memory, mind 1232, 1247.

gemynde, *adj.,* mindful 1063.

myndgian, *w.v.(2),* remember 657.

gemyndig, *adj.,* mindful 213n, 266, 818.

myngian, *w.v.(2),* [MING]; admonish 1078.

N

nāhton, *see* **āgan.**

nales, 359, **nālles,** 817, *adv.,* by no means.

nama, *m.n-stem,* name 78, 418, 465.

nāt, *see* **witan.**

nāthwylc, *pron.,* someone 73.

næfre, *adv.,* never 388.

nægel, *m.a-stem,* nail 1064, 1077, 1108, 1157; **næglan,** 1127.

nænig, *pron.,* none 505.

nære, næron, næs, *see* **wæs.**

næs, *m.a-stem,* abyss, pit 831.

ně, *neg.adv.,* not, nor 28, 221, 572.

neāh, *adv.,* nigh 66.

geneahhe, *adv.,* frequently 1064.

neān, *adv.,* clearly, close at hand 657.

nearo, *f.wō-stem,* imprisonment, difficulty 711, 1102.

nearolīc, *adj.,* grievous 912.

nearusearu, *n.wa-stem,* evil, cunning 1108.

nearusorg, *f.ō-stem,* affliction 1260.

nearwe, *adv.,* closely 1157.

neāt, *n.a-stem,* ox 357.

neāwest, *f.i-stem,* neighbourhood 67.

nēdcleofa, *see* **nȳdcleofa.**

(ge)nēgan, *w.v.(1),* address 287, 385.

(ge)nemnan, *w.v.(1),* [NEMN]; call, tell of 78, 740, 1194.

nēol, *adj.,* deep 831.

nēolnes, *f.jō-stem,* abyss 942.

neorxnawang, *m.a-stem,* Paradise 755.

nēōsan, *w.v.(1),* visit 152.

neoðan, *adv.,* [NETHEN]; from below 1114.

nēōwe, *see* **nīwe.**

generian, *w.v.(1),* save 132, 163.

nerigend, *m.cons-stem,* saviour

1077; **nergend** 461, **nergendes** 465.

nesan, v. (5), survive 1003n.

nigoða, num.adj., ninth 869, 873.

niht, f.cons-stem, night 198, 483, 694, 1227.

nihthelm, m.a-stem, cover of night 78.

nihtlang, adj., nightlong 67.

(ge)niman, v. (4), [NIM]; take 447, 599, 676, 1279.

nis, see **bēon**.

nīþ, m.a-stem, [NITH(E)]; enmity 837, 912.

niðas, m.ja-stem pl., men 465.

niðer 831, **nyðer** 942, adv., below.

nīðheard, adj., bold 195.

genīðla, m.n-stem, enmity, torment 701.

nīwe, adj., new 195, 1102; **nēowne** 869; **nīwan stefne**, afresh 1060.

nīwigan, w.v. (2), renew 940.

nō, adv., [NO¹]; never 779.

noldon, see **willan**.

nū, adv., now 313; conj., since, now that 534, 635.

nūða, adv., [NOWTHE]; just now 539.

nȳdcleofa, m.n-stem, [+CLEVE²]; prison 711; **nēdcleofan** 1275.

nȳdgefēra, m.n-stem, inevitable companion 1260n.

nȳdþearf, f.ō-stem, necessity 657.

nysse, nyste see **witan**.

nyton, see **witan**.

nyðer, see **niðer**.

O

of, prep.w.dat., of, from 75, 181, 186.

ofen, m.a-stem, furnace 1311.

ofer, prep.w.acc., over 31; after 432; in spite of 372; w.dat., upon 732.

**ofermæ
gen**, n.a-stem, superior strength 64.

oferswīðan, w.v. (1), overcome 93, 957n, 1177.

oferþearf, f.ō-stem, great need 521n.

oferwealdend, m.cons-stem, lord 1235.

ofost, f.i-stem, haste 44.

ofstlīce, adv., quickly 225.

oft, adv., often 238.

on, prep.w.acc., on 347; in 654; into 108; for 223; onto 717; w.dat., in 28; on 37; at 59; among 753; **on...gemang**, see **gemang**; **on...weard**, see **weard**.

**onæ
lan**, w.v. (1), [ANNEAL]; burn 950.

onbindan, v. (3), unbind 1249.

onbregdan, v. (3), start up 75.

onbrydan, w.v. (1), inspire 1094; **inbryrded** 841.

oncer, m.a-stem, anchor 252.

oncnāwan, v. (7), recognize 362, 965.

oncweðan, v. (5), answer 324, 573.

oncyrran, w.v. (1), change 503, 610.

oncȳðig, adj., revealing 724n.

ond, conj., and 2, 15, 20.

ondrǣdan, v. (7), dread 81.

onfōn, v. (7), [ONFANG]; receive 192, 335.

ongēan, 43, **ongēn**, 609, prep.w. dat., against, with.

onginnan, v. (3), begin 157, 303.

ongitan, v. (5), [ANGET]; understand, recognize 288, 359, 464.

onhyldan, w.v. (1), [+ HIELD]; bow 1098.

onhyrdan, w.v. (1), strengthen 840.

onlēon, v. (1), bestow 1245.

onlīce, adv. [ANLIKE a.]; similarly 99.

onlūcan, v.(2), [UNLOUK]; unlock 1250.

onmēdla, m.n-stem, pomp 1265.

onscunian, w.v.(2), reject 370.

onsendan, w.v.(1), send, yield up 120, 480, 1088.

onsīon, see **onsȳn.**

onsponnan, v.(7), open 86n.

onsȳn, f.i-stem, [ONSENE]; face 745; **onsīon** 349.

ontȳnan, w.v.(1), [UNTINE]; disclose 1229, 1248.

onwindan, v.(3), open 1249.

onwrēon, v.(1), [UNWRY]; disclose, manifest 589, 1071, 1123, 1242; **inwrige** 812.

open, adj., open 647.

geopenian, w.v.(2), open, reveal 791, 1230; **geopenigean** 1101.

orcnǣwe, adj., evident 229.

ord, m.a-stem, point, spear, beginning, best of a class 140, 235, 393, 590n, 1186; **æfter orde,** from the beginning 1154.

***orscylde,** adj., guiltless 423n.

oþ, prep.w.acc., [O³] until 139.

ōðer, adj.pron., other 233, 506, 540.

oðfæstan, w.v.(1), inflict 477.

oð/ðæt, conj., until 865.

oð/ðe, conj., or 74.

oðȳwan, see **ætywan.**

ōwiht, pron., anything 571.

P

plegean, w.v.(2), move quickly, clap the hands 245, 805n.

R

rād, f.ō-stem, journey 981.

rador, see **rodor.**

radorcyning, see **rodercining.**

rand, m.a-stem, shield 50.

raþe, see **hraðe.**

rǣd, m.a-stem, counsel, wisdom, authority 156, 553, 918, 1008.

rǣdan, v.(7), advise 1022.

gerǣde, n.ja-stem, [cp IREDE a]; equipage, agency ?, 1053n.

rǣdgeþeaht, fn.i-stem, counsel 1051.

rǣdþeahtende, pres.part., wise, deliberating 449.

rǣran, w.v.(1), raise 443, 953.

rēc, m.i-stem, smoke 794, 803.

(ge)reccan, w.v.(1), [RECCHE]; expound 281, 553, 649.

***reodian,** w.v.(2), sift 1238n.

rēonig, adj., sorrowful, 1082; **rēonian** 833.

rēonigmōd, adj., gloomy-hearted 320.

reordberend, m.cons-stem, human being 1282.

reordian, w.v.(2), [RERD(E)]; speak 405.

rēotan, v.(2), lament 1082.

gerestan, w.v.(1), cease 1082.

rīce, n.ja-stem, [RICHE]; kingdom 13, 40, 59.

rīce, adj., powerful 411; superl. 1234.

ricene, adv., quickly 607.

rīcsian, w.v.(2), [cp RIXLE]; rule 434, 773.

rīdan, v.(1), ride 50.

riht, n.a-stem, right, law, truth, judgement 372, 879, 909, 1282; **ryhte** 369.

riht, adj., true, right 13, 281; **rihte,** adv., rightly 553; **ryhte** 1074.

rīm, mn.a-stem, [RIME³]; number 2n, 284, 635.

rīmtalu, f.ō-stem, number 819.

rinc, m.a-stem, [RINK¹]; warrior 46.

rōd, f.ō-stem, cross 103, 147, 219, 482, 833, 879.

rodercining, *m.a-stem,* king of heaven *1074*n; **radorcyninges** 624; **rodorcyninges** 886.

rodor, *m.a-stem,* firmament 206, 855; **roderum, rodera** 13, 482; **radores** 794.

rōf, *adj.,* renowned 50.

gerūm, *n.a-stem,* space; **on gerūm,** away 320n.

rūm, *adj.,* spacious; *comp.* 1240.

rūn, *f.ō-stem,* [ROUN]; secret, mystery, rune, counsel 333, 411, 1261.

ryht(e), *see* **riht(e).**

gerȳman, *w.v.(1),* [+ RIME⁴]; extend 1248.

ryne, *m.i-stem,* [RUNE¹]; orbit 794.

gerȳne, *n.ja-stem,* [cp ROUN]; secret, mystery 280, 566.

S

sācerdhād, *m.a-stem,* priesthood 1054.

sacu, *f.ō-stem,* [SAKE]; strife 905, 940, 1030.

salor, *n.cons-stem,* [cp SALE¹]; hall 382.

same, some, *adv., see* **swa.**

(ge)samnian, *w.v.(2),* [SAM¹, SOMNE¹]; assemble, collect 19, 26, 55.

samod, 728, **somed,** 95, *adv.,* [SAMED]; together.

sanctus, saint 504.

sand, *n.a-stem,* sand 251n.

sang, *m.a-stem,* song 29.

sār, *n.a-stem,* wound, pain 479, 697, 940.

sāwl, *f.ō-stem,* soul 461, 889, 905, 1171.

sāwllēas, *adj.,* dead 876.

s æ, *mf.i-stem,* sea 240, 728.

sæcc, *f.jō-stem,* strife 1177.

sæcg, *see* **secg.**

sæfearoþ, *m.a-stem,* sea-shore 251.

sæl, *mf.i-stem,* [SELE]; joy 194.

sǣlan, *w.v.(1),* [SEAL²]; moor 228.

gesǣlig, *adj.,* [ISELI]; blessed 955.

sǣmearh, *m.a-stem,* ship 228, 245.

sǣne, *adj.,* reluctant 220.

sceacan, *v.(6),* [SHAKE]; hasten away 633.

(ge)scēadan, *v.(7),* [SHED]; decide, rule over(?) 149, 709.

gesceaft, *mn.a-f.i-stem,* [SHAFT¹]; creature, creation, object 183, 728, 893.

scealc, *m.a-stem,* [SHALK]; servant 692.

sceamu, *f.ō-stem,* shame 470.

gesceap, *n.a-stem,* [SHAPE]; created thing, object 789.

scēat, *m.a-stem,* [SHEET¹]; corner, place of concealment 583.

sceaða, *m.n-stem,* [SCATHE]; wretch 761, 956.

scēawian, *w.v.(2),* appear, look at 58n, 345n.

sceolu, *f.ō-stem,* [SHOAL²]; band 762.

sceððan, *v.(6),* [cp SCATHE]; harm 310.

scīnan, *w.v.(1),* shine 742, 1114.

scippend, 370, **scyppend,** 790, *m.cons-stem,* [SHEPPEND]; creator.

scīr, *adj.,* [SHIRE]; bright, radiant 310, 370.

scirian, *w.v.(1),* assign 1231.

gescrīfan, *v.(1),* [+ SHRIVE]; decree 1046.

scrīðan, *v.(1),* glide 237.

scūfan, *v.(2),* push 692.

sculan, *pret.pres.(4),* be obliged to, be necessary 210, 367, 545, 673, 763, 837, 895.

scūr, *m.a-stem,* shower 117.

scyld, *f.i-stem,* guilt 470.

scyldful, *adj.,* sinful 310.

scyldig, *adj.*, [SHILDY]; guilty 692.

scyldwyrcende, *pres.part.*, sinful 761.

scyndan, *w.v.*(*1*), hasten 30.

gescyrdan, *w.v.*(*1*), destroy 141n.,

scyppend, *see* **scippend**.

sě, sēo, þæt, 1. *pron. adj.art.*, the, that; *sg.* 11, 39, 70, 86, 93, 94, 98, 100, 185, 243, 324, 610, 925n; **sīo** 254; **sēo** 266; **þane** 294; **to þæs**, to such an extent 704; **þæs þe**, from the time when 4; **þæs**, on this account, concerning this 157, 210; **þæs þe**, because 956; **þē, þȳ**, the *with comp.* 96, 795; **to þan**, to such an extent 703; *pl.* 153, 169, 277, 285, 357, 431, 450, 652; **þan** 1127. 2. *rel. pron.*, who, which, he, she, those who, that which 101, 172, 191, 243, 398, 423, 568, 570, 709, 739n, 826, 1195n, 1201. 3. *combined with the relative particle* 154, 303, 508, 896, 974, 1161; **þæs...þe** 298.

searocræft, *m.a-stem*, cunning 1025.

searoþanc, *m.a-stem*, wisdom 414; **searuþancum** 1189.

sēaþ, *m.ua-stem*, [SEATH]; pit 693.

(ge)sēcean, *w.v.*(*1*), [ISECHE]; seek, enquire, visit 216, 230, 255, 319, 322, 325, 1179, 1280; **secean** 1148.

secg, *m.ja-stem*, [SEGGE¹]; man 47, 97, 552; **sæcg** *1256*m; **secggas** 260.

(ge)secgan, *w.v.*(*3*), [ISEGGEN]; say, speak 190, 366, 623, 665, 674, 856, 984; **secggan** 160; **gesecggan** 168.

sefa, *m.n-stem*, mind, heart 173, 376, 382.

gesēfte, *adj.*, easy to bear, *superl.* 1295.

segn, *mn.a-stem*, [SEINE²]; banner 124.

sēlest, *see* **gōd**; **sēl, sēlost**, *see* **wel**.

self, *see* **sylf**.

sellan, *w.v.*(*1*), give 182, 527; **gesyllan** 1284.

semninga, *adv.*, suddenly 1109.

sendan, *w.v.*(*1*), send 457, 930, 1199.

seofeða, *num.adj.*, seventh 697.

seofon, *num.*, seven 694.

seolf, *see* **sylf**.

seolfren, *adj.*, [SILVERN]; silver 1025.

gesēon, *v.*(*5*), [ISEE]; see 88, 1120, 1308; **geseh** 841; **gesǣgon** 68; **gesāwon** 1110; **gesīon** 243.

seonoþdōm, *m.a-stem*, assembly's decree 552.

sēpan, *w.v.*(*1*), instruct 530.

seraphin, seraphim 754.

(ge)settan, *w.v.*(*1*), place, establish, accomplish, beset 479, 495, 654, 658, 738, 1004, 1054, 1135.

gesēðan, *w.v.*(*1*), prove 581.

sīd, *adj.*, [SIDE]; broad, extensive, capacious 158, 376, 728, 1289; **sīde**, *adv.*, widely; **sīde ond wīde**, far and wide 277.

sīdweg, *m.a-stem*, distant land 282.

sige, *m.i-stem*, [SIƷE]; victory 144.

sigebēacen, *n.a-stem*, sign of victory 168, 887, 974.

sigebēam, *m.a-stem*, tree of victory 420, 846, 964, 1027.

sigebearn, *n.a-stem*, victorious son 481.

sigecwēn, *f.i-stem*, victorious queen 260.

sigelēan, *n.a-stem*, reward for victory 527.

sigelēoþ, *n.a-stem*, [+ LEOTH]; victory cry 124n.

sigeröf, *adj.*, triumphant 47, 71, 158.

sigespēd, *f.i-stem*, victory 1171.

sigor, *m.os-a-stem,* victory 85, 346, *1180*n, 1182.

sigorbēācen, *n.a-stem,* sign of victory 984.

sigorcynn, *n.ja-stem,* victorious race 754.

sigorlēan, *n.a-stem,* reward of victory 623.

gesihþ, *f.ō-stem,* sight 614; **gesyhþ** 98; **gesyhðe** 184n.

sinc, *n.a-stem,* treasure 194.

sincgim, *m.a-stem,* jewel 264.

sincweorðung, *f.ō-stem,* costly gift 1218.

sindrēam, *m.a-stem,* eternal joy 740.

singāl, *adj.*, perpetual 905.

singāllīce, *adv.*, perpetually 746.

singan, *v.(3),* sing 109, 337, 746, 1153.

siomian, *w.v.(2),* abide 694.

(ge)sīōn, *see* **(ge)sēon**.

sionoþ, *m.a-stem,* assembly 154.

sioððan, *see* **siððan**.

(ge)sittan, *v.(5),* sit 731, 867.

sīþ, *m.a-stem,* [SITHE¹]; journey, experience, time 111, 247, 817, 910, 1000.

sīþ, *adv.*, late 74.

sīðdæg, *m.a-stem,* later time 639.

sīöfæt, *mn.a-stem,* journey 220, 229.

sīðian, *w.v.(2),* [SITHE¹]; journey 95.

siððan, *adv.*, [SITHEN]; afterwards, since 271, 636; **sioððan**, 1146; *conj.*, when 230; **syððan**, from the time when 116; **syð-ðan**, from the time when 116; **syððan furðum**, *see* **furðum**.

slæp, *m.a-stem,* sleep 69.

slīðe, *adj.*, cruel 856.

smǣte, *adj.*, [SMEAT]; refined 1309.

smēagan, *w.v.(2),* consider 413.

snottor, *adj.*, [SNOTER]; wise 1189; *superl.* **snoterestum** 277.

snūde, *adv.*, quickly 154.

snyrgan, *w.v.(1),* hasten 244.

snyttro, *f.ō-stem,* wisdom 154, 293.

some, *see* **same**.

somed, *see* **samod**.

sōna, *adv.*, forthwith 47, 85, 222.

sorg, *f.ō-stem,* sorrow 694, 921, 1030.

sorgian, *w.v.(2),* sorrow 1081.

sorglēas, *adj.*, joyful; *comp.* 97.

sōþ, *n.a-stem,* truth 307, 395; **tō sōðe**, of a truth 160.

sōþ, *adj.*, true 461, 777, 887, 891.

sōðcwide, *m.i-stem,* true saying 530.

sōðcyning, *m.a-stem,* true king 444.

sōðfæst, *adj.*, pious 7, 1289.

sōðfæstnes, *f.jō-stem,* faith, piety 1148.

sōðlīce, *adv.*, truly 200.

sōðwundor, *n.a-stem,* true wonder 1121.

spāld, *n.a-stem,* [SPOLD]; spittle 300.

spēd, *f.i-stem,* success, abundance 366, 1181.

spēowan, *w.v.(1),* spew 297.

spild, *m.cons-stem,* destruction 1118.

gespon, *n.a-stem,* [cp SPAN²]; clasp, link 1134n.

spōwan, *v.(7),* succeed 916.

(ge)sprecan, *v.(5),* speak 332, 667, 1285.

stærcedfyrhþ, *adj.*, resolute 38.

stæþ, *n.a-stem,* [STAITHE]; bank, shore 38, 60.

stān, *m.a-stem,* stone 492, 565, 613, 615.

stānclif, *n.a-stem,* rock, cliff 135.

standan, *v.(6),* stand, rise 113, 227, 232, 577.

stāngefōg, *n.a-stem,* mason's art 1020.

stāngripe, *m.i-stem, see* **worpian.**

stānhlīþ, *n.a-stem,* [+ LITH²]; cliff; **stanhlēōðum,** 653.

staðelian, *w.v.(2),* [STATHEL]; make firm, establish 427, 796; **staðolian,** 1093.

stæppan, *v.(6),* advance, move 121.

gesteald, *n.a-stem,* dwelling 801.

stēām, *m.a-stem,* steam, vapour 802.

stearc, *adj.,* [STARK]; hard, obstinate 565, 615n.

stede, *m.i-stem,* place 135.

stedewang, *m.a-stem,* place 675.

stefn, *f.ō-stem,* [STEVEN¹]; voice 747.

stefn, [STEVEN²]; *see* **nīwe.**

stēnan, *see* 151n.

stīðhycgende, *pres.part.,* [STITH +]; bold, 683, 716.

stīðhīdig, *adj.,* resolute 121.

stōw, *f.wō-stem,* place 653, 675, 683, 716.

strang, *adj.,* strong 703.

strēām, *m.a-stem,* stream 1200.

strūdan, *v.(2),* rob 904.

stunde, *adv.,* [cp STOUND sb.¹]; forthwith 723.

stundum, *adv.,* [STUNDUM]; at times 121.

sum, *pron. adj.,* a certain one 131, 132, 479.

sumer, *m.ua-stem,* summer 1227.

sund, *n.a-stem,* [SOUND¹]; sea 228.

gesund, *adj.,* safe 996.

sundor, *adv.,* apart 407.

sundorwīs, *adj.,* singularly wise 588.

sunne, *f.n-stem,* sun 1109.

sunu, *m.u-stem,* son 222, 447, 474, 1199.

sūsl, *n.a-f.ō-stem,* torture 771, 943, 949.

swā, *adv.,* so, thus 163, 271; such 541; like, as 1309; **swā some, same,** likewise 653, 1206; *conj.,* when, as, as soon as 87, 100; as far as 971; **swā...swā þēah,** although...yet 498–500; **swā ...swā,** either...or 325; *rel.* who 190; **swā þæs,** whose 340.

swǣs, *adj.,* dear 447.

swāmian, *w.v.(2),* grow dark 629n.

sweart, *adj.,* [SWART]; black; *superl.* 930.

swefan, *v.(5),* [SWEVE]; sleep 70.

swefen, *n.a-stem,* dream 71.

swegl, *n.a-stem,* heaven 75, 507.

*****swelling,** *f.ō-stem,* swelling sail 245n.

sweng, *m.i-stem,* blow 239.

gesweorcan, *v.(3),* [SWERK]; darken 855.

sweord, *n.a-stem,* sword 756.

sweordgenīðla, *m.n-stem,* enemy 1180.

swēōt, *n.a-stem,* troop 124n.

sweotole, *adv.,* [cp SUTEL *a.*]; clearly 26.

sweotollīce, *adv.,* clearly 690.

geswerigan, *w.v.(1),* swear 686.

geswīcan, *v.(1),* [ISWIKE]; desist 516.

swīge, *adj.,* [cp SWIE v.]; still 1274.

swilt, 677, **swylt,** 447, *m.i-stem,* death.

swinsian, *w.v.(2),* resound 240.

swīþra, *comp. adj.,* [SWITHER]; right 347.

swīðe, *adv.,* [SWITH]; greatly 663; *superl.* 668.

geswiðrian, *w.v.(2),* [cp SWITHER¹]; diminish 698, 1263.

swonrād, *f.ō-stem*, sea 996.

swylc, *pron.*, such 571; which 32; swylce, *adv.*, likewise 3; as it were 1112.

swylt, *see* swilt.

syb, *f.jō-stem*, [SIB²]; kindred, tribe, peace 26, 446, 598, 1182.

ģesyhþ, *see* ģesihþ.

sylf, *pron.*, self 69, 200, 222, 303, 1000, 1206, 1295; seolfe 1120; selfre 1199; seolfne 488.

ģesyllan, *see* sellan.

symle, *adv.*, always 469.

syn, *f.jō-stem*, sin 414, 497, 677, 771.

ģesȳne, *adj.*, visible 144, 264.

synful, *adj.*, sinful 1295.

synniġ, *adj.*, sinful 955.

synwyrcende, *pres.part.*, sinful 395, 943.

syððan, *see* siððan.

syx, *num.*, six 740, 741.

syxta, *num.adj.*, sixth 7.

T

tācen, *n.a-stem*, symbol 85, 164, 171, 184; heroic deed 645n; remarkable event 319; tācnum, *adv.*, clearly 853.

ģetācnian, *w.v.(2)*, show forth 753.

(ġe)tǣcan, *w.v.(1)*, teach, show 601, 631, 1074.

tēar, *m.a-stem*, tear 1133.

(ġe)tellan, *w.v.(1)*, suppose, count 2n; talde 908.

tempel, *n.a-stem*, temple 1009, 1021, 1057.

ģetenġan, *w.v.(1)*, apply oneself 200.

ģetenġe, *adj.*, near to 228, 1113.

tēona, *m.n-stem*, [TEEN¹]; vexation 987.

tīd, *f.i-stem*, time, hour 193, 873, 1043; tīdum, *adv.*, at times 1248.

til, *adj.*, good 325.

ģetimbran, *w.v.(1)*, [TIMBER]; build 1009.

tīonlēġ, *mn.i-stem*, destroying flame 1279.

tīr, *m.a-stem*, glory 164, 753.

tīrēadiġ, *adj.*, glorious 104, 605.

tō, *prep.w.dat.*, to 32; as 10; of 319; with the inflected infinitive 533, *adv.*, too 63; to 1104.

tōġēnes, *prep.w.dat.*, [TOGAINS]; towards, in reply 167, 536.

tōġlīdan, *v.(1)*, depart 78, 1268.

tohte, *f.n-stem*, battle 1179.

torht, *n.a-stem*, brightness 1248.

torht, *adj.*, bright; *superl.* 164.

torn, *n.a-stem*, grief 1133.

tornġenīðla, *m.n-stem*, bitter foe 568.

tōsomne, *adv.*, [TOSAME]; together 1201.

tōweorpan, *v.(3)*, destroy 430.

tōwrecan, *v.(5)*, scatter 131.

trāġ, *f.ō-stem*, affliction 668.

trāġ, *adj.*, evil 325, 954.

tredan, *v.(5)*, tread 55, 612.

trēo, *n.wa-stem*, tree 107, 706, 1026, 1251; trīo 429; trēow 664.

trymman, *w.v.(1)*, [TRIM]; confirm, draw up in formation 14, 35n.

ģetrȳwe, *adj.*, faithful 1034.

turfhaga, *m.n-stem*, [+ HAW¹]; sod 829.

twēġen, *num.*, two 2, 853, 879, 1306.

twēntiġ, *num.*, twenty 829.

twēo, *m.n-stem*, doubt 171, 668.

tyht, *m.i-stem*, [TIGHT¹]; march, motion 53.

ģetȳn, *w.v.(1)*, teach 1017.

ģetȳnan, *w.v.(1)*, [TINE¹]; enclose 721, 920.

þ

þā, *adv.*, [THO]; then 1, 7, *conj.*, when 389; þā gīna, *see* gīna.

þafian, *w.v.*(2), [THAVE]; consent 608.

þanc, *m.a-stem*, thanks 810.

geþanc, *mn.a-stem*, thought 267, 1238; geþonc 1286.

þancian, *w.v.*(2), thank 961.

þanon, *adv.*, [THENNE]; thence 143.

þǣr, *adv.*, there, then 41, 84; *conj.*, where, if 70, 838, *adv.*, would that 978n.

þæt, *conj.*, so that 15; that 144; in order that 375; because 59n,175.

þe, *rel.pron.*, who, which, where 160, 577, 717n; *comp.rel.* 1278.

þēah, *conj.*, though 48.

þeaht, *f.ō-stem*, thought 1241.

geþeaht, *fn.i-stem*, counsel, knowledge 468, 1240.

þeahtian, *w.v.*(2), take counsel 547.

þearf, *f.ō-stem*, [THARF]; need 426.

þearl, *adj.*, severe 704.

þēaw, *m.wa-stem*, [THEW[1]]; custom, *pl.* morality 1210.

þegn, *m.a-stem*, thane, servant, retainer 151, 487, 540.

þegnung, *f.ō-stem*, service 738, 744.

(ge)þencan, *w.v.*(1), think, consider 296, 313, 549.

þēod, *f.ō-stem*, [THEDE]; nation 185, 448, 539.

þēodcwēn, *f.i-stem*, empress 1155.

þēoden, *m.a-stem*, prince 267, 487.

þēodenbealu, *n.wa-stem*, terrible evil 403.

þēodscipe, *m.i-stem*, instruction 1166.

þēosterloca, *m.n-stem*, tomb 485.

þēostorcofa, *m.n-stem*, [+ COVE[1]]; dark chamber 832.

þēostre, *adj.*, [THESTER]; dark 312.

þēostru, *f.ō-stem*, [THESTER]; darkness 766; þȳstrum 307.

þēowdōm, *m.a-stem*, service 201.

þēownēd, *f.i-stem*, bondage 769.

þerscan, *v.*(3), [THRASH]; beat 358.

þes, *adj.pron.*, this, 92, 162, 312, 402, 468, 576, 630, 700, 703, 748, 857, 905 (*see note to* 161), 1172.

þicgan, *v.*(5), [THIG]; receive 1258.

þīn, *adj.*, thy, thine 510, 597, 666, 726, 738, 766, 769, 772, 928, 1088.

þincan, *see* þyncan.

þing, *n.a-stem*, thing, condition 409, 608n.

geþinge, *n.ja-stem*, fate 253.

þinggemearc, *n.a-stem*, period of time 3n.

þingian, *w.v.*(2), speak, intercede 77, 494.

geþōht, *mn.a-stem*, thought 426.

(ge)þolian, *w.v.*(2), [THOLE]; endure 769, 1292.

geþonc, *see* geþanc.

þonne, *adv.*, then 50, 446; *conj.*, when 473; than 74; þone 49; since 1177.

þracu, *f.ō-stem*, attack 45.

þrǣcheard, *adj.*, brave 123.

þrǣgan, *w.v.*(1), run 1262.

þrāgum, *adv.*, [cp THROW sb.[1]]; at times 1238.

þrēa, *f.wō-mn.a-stem*, violence 1276.

(ge)þrēagan, *w.v.*(2), [THREA]; torment 321, 1296.

þrēalīc, *adj.*, terrible 426.

þrēanȳd, *f.i-stem*, cruel necessity 704; þrēanēdum 883.

þrēat, *m.a-stem*, [THREAT]; band 51, 546.

geþrēatian, *w.v.*(2), torment 695.

geþrec, *n.a-stem,* press, tumult 114.

þreodian, *see* **þrydian.**

þridda, *num.adj.,* third 185, 854, 883.

þrīe, *num.,* three 2, 483, 846, 857, 1286.

(ge)þringan, *v.(3),* [THRING]; press forward, throng 40, 123, 329.

þrīste, *adj.,* [THRISTE]; bold, presumptuous 267, 1286; *adv.,* 409.

þrittig, *num.,* thirty 3.

þroht, *m.a-stem,* affliction 704.

þrohtherd, *adj.,* patient 494.

þrosm, *m.a-stem,* vapour 1298.

(ge)þrōwian, *w.v.(2),* [THROW²]; suffer 421, 519, 563, 768, 854.

þrydian, *w.v.(2),* deliberate 549; **þreodude** 1238.

þrym, *m.i-stem,* [THRUM¹]; glory 177, 348, 483, 1089.

þrymcyning, *m.a-stem,* king of glory 494.

þrymlīce, *adv.,* gloriously 780.

þrymsittende, *pres.part,* enthroned in glory 810.

þrȳnes, *f.jō-stem,* trinity 177.

þrȳðbord, *n.a-stem,* mighty shield, ship? 151n.

þū, *pron.,* thou 79, 81, 82, 83, 403, 927.

þūf, *m.a-stem,* banner of plumes 123.

þurfan, *pret.pres.(3),* [THARF]; need 918, 939, 1103.

þurh, *prep.w.acc.,* through, in, because of; 6, 1236n; **þurg** 289; on account of 400.

þurhdrīfan, *v.(1),* permeate 707.

þurhgēotan, *v.(2),* [+ YET]; endue 961.

þurhwadan, *v.(6),* pierce 1065.

þus, *adv.,* thus 189.

þūsend, *num.,* thousand 285, 326.

þyder, *adv.,* thither 548.

þȳlæs, *conj.,* lest 430.

þyncan, *w.v.(1),* seem 72, 541, 1164; **þince** 532.

þyslīc, *adj.,* such 540, 546.

þȳstru, *see* **þēostru.**

U

ūhta, *m.n-stem,* [UGHTEN]; dawn 105.

unāsecgendlīc, *adj.,* ineffable 466.

unbrǣce, *adj.,* inviolable *1028n.*

unclǣne, *adj.,* unclean 301.

uncūþ, *adj.,* unknown 1101.

uncȳðig, *adj.,* ignorant ? 960n.

undearninga, *adv.,* plainly 405; **undearnunga** 620.

under, *prep.w.acc.dat.,* under 13, 763.

ungelīce, *adv.,* [UNILICHE]; differently 1307.

unhwīlen, *adj.,* eternal 1231.

unlifgende, *pres.part.,* lifeless 878.

unlȳtel, *adj.,* great, much 283, 871.

unoferswīðed, *past part.,* invincible 1187.

unriht, *n.a-stem,* wrong 472.

unriht, *adj.,* wrong 1041.

unrīme, *adj.,* numberless 61.

unscyldig, *adj.,* guiltless 496.

unscynde, *adj.,* noble 365, 1200.

unslāw, *adj.,* quick 202.

unsnyttro, *f.ō-stem,* folly 946, 1285.

unsōfte, *adv.,* with difficulty 132.

untrāglīce, *adv.,* honestly 410.

untwēonde, *adj.,* unwavering 797.

unweaxen, *past part.,* young 529.

unwīslīce, *adv.,* foolishly 293.

up, *adv.,* up 87.

uppan, *prep.w.dat.,* upon 885.

uppe, *adv.,* aloft 52.

uprador, *m.a-stem,* firmament 730.

upweard, *adv.,* upward 805.

ūrigfeðera, 29, **ūrigfeðra,** 111, *adj.,* dewy-feathered.

ūser, *adj.,* our 425.

ūt, *adv.,* out 45.

ūðweota, *m.n-stem,* [UÞWITE]; wise man, elder 473.

W

wā, *adv.,* ill 628.

(ge)wadan, *v.*(6), go 246, 1189.

waldan, *see* **wealdan.**

waldend, *see* **wealdend.**

wan, *adj.,* dark 53.

wang, *m.a-stem,* [WONG]; place 684.

wansǣlig, *adj.,* accursed 977; **wonsǣlige** 478.

wangstede, *m.i-stem,* place 793.

wannhāl, *adj.,* infirm 1029.

wǣdl, *f.ō-stem,* [WÆDLE]; want 617.

wǣg, *m.i-stem,* [cp WAW¹]; wave 230.

wǣgflota, *m.n-stem,* [+FLOTE¹]; ship 245.

wǣghengest, *m.a-stem,* ship 236.

gewǣlan, *w.v.*(1), afflict 1243.

wælfel, *adj.,* fierce 53.

wælhlence, *f.n-stem,* coat-of-mail 24.

wælhrēow, *adj.,* cruel 112.

wælrest, *f.jō-stem,* place of rest on the battle field 723.

wælrūn, *f.ō-stem,* slaughter rune 28.

wǣpen, *n.a-stem,* weapon 17, 48, 1188.

wǣpenþracu, *f.ō-stem,* battle 106.

wǣr, *f.ō-stem,* [WARE⁴]; covenant, pledge 80, 822.

wǣrlīc, *adj.,* cunning 544.

wæs, wǣre, *p.t.sg.,* was, were in 1, 7, 159, 707, 776, 990; *pl.* were 22, 291.

wæstm, *mn.a-f.ō-stem,* [WASTUM]; increase 341.

wæter, *n.a-stem,* water 39.

wǣðan, *w.v.*(1), hunt 1273.

wē, *pron.,* we 364, 397, 399, 400, 533, 637.

wēadǣd, *f.i-stem,* deed bringing sorrow 495.

weald, *m.ua-stem,* forest 28.

geweald, *mn.a-stem,* [IWALD]; power 120, 610.

wealdan, *v.*(7), rule 450, 760; **walde** 800.

wealdend, *m.cons-stem,* [WALD-END]; ruler 4,391; **waldend** 731.

weallan, *v.*(7), [WALL¹]; be fervent 937.

weard, *m.a-stem,* guardian 153, 384, 1100.

weard, [-WARD]; *in* on... **weard,** towards 84.

weardian, *w.v.*(2), maintain, guard 135, 1144.

wearhtræf, *n.a-stem,* [WARY +]; hell 926.

weaxan, *v.*(7), grow 12, 547n, 913.

webbian, *w.v.*(2), contrive 309.

wed, *n.ja-stem,* pledge; **wed gesyllan,** be responsible for 1284.

wēdan, *w.v.*(1), [WEDE]; rage 1273.

wefan, *v.*(5), weave, contrive 1237.

weg, *m.a-stem,* way 1149.

wegan, *v.*(5), [WEIGH¹]; feel 61.

wel, *adv.,* well; *comp.* **sēl** 795; *superl.* **sēlest** 374; **sēlost** 1157.

wēmend, *m.cons-stem,* one who reveals 879.

wēna, *m.n-stem,* expectation 584.

wēnan, *w.v.*(1), expect 62, 478, 668, 1103.

(ge)wendan, *w.v.*(1), change, turn away, depart *348,* 440, 617, 978, 1046,

weorc, *n.a-stem*, work 110, 1242, 1318.

weorod, weorud, *see* **werod**.

weorpan, *v.(3)*, [WARP]; cast 1304.

(ge)weorðan, *v.(3)*, [WORTH¹]; become, be, happen 5, 130, 220, 336, 401, 428, 429, 456, 575, 614n, 632, 643, 922, 960, 975, 1191, 1288.

(ge)weorðian, *w.v.(2)*, [WORTH²]; honour 150, 177, 822, 890, 1136, 1221.

weoruld, *see* **woruld**.

wer, *m.a-stem* [WERE¹]; man 22, 72, 236, 287, 304, 508, 784.

wergan, *w.v.(1)*, [WARY]; curse 294.

wergðu, *f.ō-stem*, damnation 211, 295, 309.

gewerian, *w.v.(1)*, clothe 263.

wěrig, *adj.*, weary, wretched 357, 387, 762; *cp Beo. ed. Klaeber 133*n.

werod, *n.a-stem*, [WERED]; host; army 19, 39, 48, 53, 230, **weor(u)da** 223, 1149n; **weorodum** 351; **wereda** 1084.

werodlēst, *f.ō-stem*, lack of troops 63.

werþēod, *f.ō-stem*, nation 17, 643, 968.

westan, *adv.*, [WESTEN]; from the west 1015.

wēsten, *n.ja-stem*, wilderness 611.

wīc, *n.a-f.ō-stem*, [WICK²]; dwelling-place 1037.

wicg, *n.ja-stem*, [WIDGE]; steed 1195.

wīcian, *w.v.(2)*, [WICK¹]; encamp 38, 65.

wīd, *adj.*, wide, far; **wīde** *adv.*, widely 131; **on wīdan fēore, to wīdan fēore**, *see* **feorh**; **wīdan fyrhþ**, *see* **fyrhþ**.

wīf, *n.a-stem*, woman 223, 236, 1131.

wīg, *n.a-stem*, [WI]; warfare 19, 112, 131; **wīgges** 824; **wīgge** 48.

wiga, *m.n-stem*, [WYE¹]; warrior 63, 246, 344.

*****wiga**, *m.n-stem*, the Holy Spirit ? 937n.

wīgend, *m.cons-stem*, warrior 106; **wīggende** 983.

wīgspēd, *f.i-stem*, success in battle 165.

wīgþracu, *f.ō-stem*, strife 430; **wīggþræce** 658.

wiht, *fn.i-stem*, something 684.

wilfægen, *adj.*, joyful 827.

wilgifa, *see* **willgifa**.

willa, *m.n-stem*, joy, will, desire 267, 681, 772; **Dryhtne to willan**, for the Lord's sake 193; **Criste to willan**, for Christ's sake 678.

willan, *anom.v.*, be willing, intend 40, 219, 394, 420, 469, 566, 574, 608, 621, 1079, 1180.

willgifa, *m.n-stem*, ruler 814, 1111; **wilgifan** 221.

willhrēðig, *adj.*, exultant 1116.

willsīþ, *m.a-stem*, joyful errand 223.

willspell, *n.a-stem*, joyful news 993; **wilspella** 983.

wind, *m.a-stem*, wind 1271.

winemæg, *m.a-stem*, kinsman 1015.

winter, *mn.ua-stem*, winter, year 4.

wintergerīm, *n.a-stem*, number of years 654.

wīr, *m.a-stem*, wire, filigree work 1134n, 1263.

wīs, *adj.*, wise 592; *superl.* 153, 169, 323.

wīsdōm, *m.a-stem*, wisdom 334, 357, 1242.

wīse, *f.n-stem,* matter 684.

wīsfæst, *adj.,* wise 314.

wist, *f.i-stem* [WIST]; food 617.

wita, *m.n-stem,* [WITE¹]; wise man 544.

witan, *pret.pres.(1),* know 401n, 419, 459n, 640, 644, 719, 859, 945, 1239.

wītan, *v.(1),* [WITE¹]; accuse 416.

gewītan, *v.(1),* [IWITE]; depart 94, 1271, 1277.

wīte, *n.ja-stem,* [WITE²]; torment 180, 520, 764.

wītebrōga, *m.n-stem,* terrible punishment 931.

wītedōm, *m.a-stem,* prophecy 1152.

wītga, *m.n-stem,* [WITIE]; wise man, prophet 289, *561,* 592, 1188.

gewitt, *n.ja-stem,* understanding 357, 937.

wiþ, *prep.w.acc.,* towards 822; against 403; *w.gen.,* against 616; *w.dat.,* with 307; to 77; against 18.

wiðercyr *m.i-stem,* [+ CHARE¹]; reversal 925.

wiðerhycgende, *pres.part.,* malevolent 951.

wiðersæc, *n.a-stem,* contradiction 569.

wiðhyccgan, *w.v.(3),* scorn 618.

wiðrēotan, *v.(2),* oppose 369n.

wiðsacan, *v.(6),* [WITHSAKE]; deny, refuse, renounce 390, 617, 663, 766, 932, 1039, 1121.

wiðweorpan, *v.(3),* spurn 294.

wlanc, *adj.,* [WLONK]; proud 231.

gewlencan, *w.v.(1),* [WLENCH]; adorn 1263.

wlītan, *v.(1),* look 385.

wlite, *m.i-stem,* [WLITE]; glory 1319.

wlitescȳne, *adj.,* beautiful 72.

wlitig, *adj.,* [WLITI]; beautiful 77, 165; **wliti** 89; *superl.* 748.

wolcen, *n.a-stem,* [WELKIN]; cloud 89, 1271.

wom, *mn.a-stem,* [WAM]; sin, stain 583.

wōma, *m.n-stem,* harbinger, revelation, sound of battle 19n, 71.

womful, *adj.,* sinful 760.

womsceaða, *m.n-stem,* sinner 1299.

wonhȳdig, *adj.,* foolish 762.

wonsælig, *see* **wansælig.**

wōp, *m.a-stem,* lamentation 1131.

word, *n.a-stem,* word 24n, 221, 314, *338,* 544, 581, 945.

wordcræft, *m.a-stem,* eloquence 592, 1237n.

wordcwide, *m.i-stem,* speech 547.

wordgerȳne, *n.ja-stem,* mystic saying 289.

worn, *m.a-stem,* great number 633.

worpian, *w.v.(2),* throw; **stānum, stāngreopum worpian,** stone 492, 823–4.

woruld, *f.i-stem,* world 508, 1141, *1276;* **worlde** 993; **in woruld weorulda,** for ever and ever 452.

woruldgedāl, *n.a-stem,* death 581.

woruldrīce, 456, **worldrīce** 1048, *n.ja-stem,* earthly kingdom.

woruldstund, *f.ō-stem,* time in the world; **æfter woruldstundum,** in the world 363.

wōþ, *f.ō-stem,* song 748.

wracu, *f.ō-stem,* [WRAKE¹]; retribution, misery 17, 495.

wrāþ, *adj.,* wroth, hostile 165, 459, 1181.

wrāðe, *adv.,* [WROTHE]; perversely 294.

wraðu, *f.ō-stem,* help, support 84, 1029.

wræcmæcg, *m.ja-stem,* [WRACK[1] +]; outcast, wretch; **wræcmæcggas** 387

wrǣtlīce, *adv.,* wondrously; *superl.* 1019.

wrecan, *v.(5),* press forward 121.

wreccan, *w.v.(1),* [WRECCHE]; rouse 106.

wrēon, *(v.1),* [WRY[1]]; conceal 583.

gewrit, *n.a-stem,* writing, Scripture 387, 674, 826.

wrīðan, *v.(1),* [WRITHE]; weave 24.

wrixlan, *w.v.(1),* [WRIXLE]; change 758.

wrōht, *m.a-f.ō-stem,* slander 309.

wrōhtstæf, *m.a-stem,* calumny 925.

wuldor, *n.a-stem,* [WULDER]; glory 5, 77, 295, 812, *1134*n.

wuldorcyning, *m.a-stem,* king of glory 291, 1321.

wuldorfæst, *adj.,* glorious 966.

wuldorgeofa, *m.n-stem,* giver of glory 681.

wuldorgifu, *f.ō-stem,* glorious gift 1071.

wulf, *m.a-stem,* wolf 28.

wund, *f.ō-stem,* wound 514.

wundor, *n.a-stem,* miracle 363, 826, 866, 1237.

wundorwyrd, *f.i-stem,* wonderful event 1070.

wundrian, *w.v.(2),* marvel 958.

(ge)wunigan, *w.v.(2),* [WON]; dwell, inhabit 624, 723, 820, 949, 1027, 1037.

wylm, *m.i-stem,* [WALM[1]]; swell, surging fire 39, 764, 1299.

wyn, *f.i-stem,* joy 788, 1039, 1089.

wynbēam, *m.a-stem,* tree of joy 843.

wynsum, *adj.,* joyful 793.

(ge)wyrcan, *w.v.(1),* [IWURCHE]; work, construct, perform 104, 470, 513, 726, 826, 1019.

(ge)wyrd, *f.i-stem,* [WEIRD]; Providence, event, fact 80, 541, 647, 812n, 1046.

wyrdan, *w.v.(1),* [WERDE]; destroy 903.

wyrrest, wyrsa, *see* yfel.

wyrðe, *adj.,* [WURTHE]; precious 291.

Y

yfel, *n.a-stem,* evil 493, 901.

yfel, *adj.,* evil; *comp.,* 1039; *superl.* 931.

yfemest, *superl.adj.,* [UVEMEST]; uppermost 1290.

ylde, *see* ilde.

ymb, *prep.w.acc.,* [UMBE]; around, by 39, 136; concerning 214; after 272.

ymbhwyrft, *m.i-stem,* orb, firmament 730.

ymbsellan, *w.v.(1),* surround 741.

ymbsittend, *m.cons-stem,* neighbour 33.

yppe, *adj.,* [cp UPPE v.]; known 435.

yrfe, *n.ja-stem,* [ERF[1]]; heritage 1320.

yrmðu, *f.ō-stem,* [ERMTH(E)]; misery 952; **ermðum** 767.

yrre, *adj.,* [IRRE]; angry 573; **eorne** 685.

ȳþ, *f.jō-stem,* [YTHE]; wave 239.

ȳðhof, *n.a-stem,* ship *252*n.

geȳwan, *w.v.(1),* reveal 488; **gehȳwdest** 786; **geīewed** 102.

INDEX OF PROPER NAMES